M000282175

Praise for *When the Lord Speaks to Your Heart*

"Father Gaston Courtois (1897–1970) is one of the great spiritual theologians and writers of the twentieth century. *When the Lord Speaks to Your Heart* is Father Courtois' reflection on his joyful, living, and radiant life of prayer. The writing is done in such a way that it is God speaking tenderly and compassionately to the person reading and praying: 'Call upon me. Love me. Let yourself be flooded with the conviction of being passionately loved as you are, with all your limitations and your miseries, so that you may become what I desire you to be: the living, burning coals of divine charity.' Those who pick up this book will find themselves being apprenticed, mentored, and inspired by a master contemplative missionary completely devoted to the Catholic Church's evangelizing mission on earth."

— *John O. Barres, Bishop of Allentown*

"In *When the Lord Speaks to Your Heart*, Father Courtois records the words of the Lord as he heard them. The selections draw me closer to Jesus, strengthening me for daily living. And they persuade me that the Lord will also speak to my heart if only I will seek him more faithfully and listen to him more carefully."

—*Bert Ghezzi, author of* The Power of Daily Prayer

WHEN THE LORD SPEAKS TO YOUR HEART

WHEN THE LORD SPEAKS TO YOUR HEART

DAILY REFLECTIONS

By Gaston Courtois

Translated by Aloysius Owen, SJ

Foreword by James R. Mattaliano, SJ

Pauline
BOOKS & MEDIA
Boston

Library of Congress Cataloging-in-Publication Data

Names: Courtois, Gaston, author.

Title: When the Lord speaks to your heart : daily reflections / Gaston Courtois ; translated by Aloysius Owen, SJ.

Other titles: Quand le Seigneur parle au coeur. English

Description: Boston, MA : Pauline Books & Media, 2016. | "Originally published in French as Quand le Seigneur parle au coeur."

Identifiers: LCCN 2016023604| ISBN 9780819883698 (pbk.) | ISBN 0819883697 (pbk.)

Subjects: LCSH: Meditations.

Classification: LCC BX2183 .C6313 2016 | DDC 242--dc23

LC record available at https://lccn.loc.gov/2016023604

Originally published in French as *Quand le Seigneur parle au coeur* by Éditions Médiaspaul, Paris, copyright © 1991, Éditions Paulines, Sherbooke, QC.

Translated by Aloysius Owen, SJ

Adapted by the Daughters of St. Paul

The Scripture quotations contained herein are from the *New Revised Standard Version Bible: Catholic Edition*, copyright © 1989, 1993, Division of Christian Education of the National Council of the Churches of Christ in the United States of America. Used by permission. All rights reserved.

Cover design by Rosana Usselmann

Cover art: D. Velazquez, *Supper at Emmaus*

All rights reserved. No part of this book may be reproduced or transmitted in any form or by any means, electronic or mechanical, including photocopying, recording, or by any information storage and retrieval system, without permission in writing from the publisher.

"P" and PAULINE are registered trademarks of the Daughters of St. Paul.

Edition copyright © 2016, Daughters of St. Paul

Published by Pauline Books & Media, 50 Saint Paul's Avenue, Boston, MA 02130-3491

www.pauline.org

Printed in the U.S.A.

Pauline Books & Media is the publishing house of the Daughters of St. Paul, an international congregation of women religious serving the Church with the communications media.

2 3 4 5 6 7 8 9   21 20 19 18 17

Contents

Foreword

At the very beginning of his autobiography, *Confessions*, Saint Augustine, addressing and praising the Lord in prayer, acknowledges: "You have made us for yourself and our hearts are restless until they find rest in you" (bk. 1, chap. 1). In expressing this, Augustine recognizes the reality of our human existence as being completely dependent upon God who is the fulfillment of all our hopes and desires. Centuries before, King David expressed a similar sentiment when composing Psalm 62: "For God alone my soul waits in silence; / from him comes my salvation" (62:1). Saint Ignatius of Loyola likewise states in the "Principle and Foundation" of the *Spiritual Exercises* that "man is created to praise, reverence, and serve God our Lord, and by this means to save his soul." All of these attest to the great longing of the human heart to be in relationship with God who is the source of our life and our hope.

Humanity was created for relationship. We were all created to be in relationship with God as he is in relationship with

himself and with us. Further, we were all created to be in relationship with one another. It is only from living out of this relationship
that we find fulfillment and life everlasting. *When the Lord Speaks
to Your Heart* by Father Gaston Courtois is precisely about this
relationship and God's invitation to enter into and grow in intimate friendship with him.

In my studies in preparation for ordination to the priesthood,
one of my professors posited that when God created us in his
image and likeness, we were created immediately in his image, but
creation in his likeness would be a lifelong process. It is the most
fundamental and important pursuit of our lives as we continually
conform our lives to his, our words and actions to his, our wills to
his, and our hearts to his. Saint Augustine experienced this deep
longing in his heart as he sought the Lord to fulfill this yearning.
We are all called to rest our hearts in the heart of the Lord. Our
hearts ache for this relationship, even if we are unaware of it.

Do we desire this? Do we cry out to God, seeking him with
the deep longing and thirst that are depicted in Psalms 63 and 42?
Are we willing to enter into a deeper and more intimate relationship with the Lord who constantly beckons us to draw closer? If
our response is like that of Augustine, David, Ignatius, and so
many others, the question then arises as to how this can be
achieved. How can we grow into that deeper, more intimate, and
ever richer relationship with the Lord?

First and foremost, we must listen. We must quiet ourselves
in order to go within our hearts to where the Lord speaks—quietly, softly, tenderly, and with much love. We must attend to the
"still small voice" (see 1 Kings 19:12) where deep calls to deep (Ps

42:7) so that heart can speak to heart. To grow deeper in intimacy with God is to allow ourselves to hunger and thirst for his word while ever longing to seek his presence.

His thoughts must become our thoughts. Thoughts enkindle desires; desires motivate and move us to action. Before a word or action comes into being it exists first as a thought. Words and actions are the perfections of thought. Our thoughts will either nurture our hearts to draw closer to God and the good, or harden our hearts and withdraw them from God, moving them toward evil. We must therefore open our hearts to seek God's Spirit who will speak to them. As the Apostle James encourages us in his letter (4:8): "draw near to God and he will draw near to you."

The very rich reflections that are contained within Father Gaston Courtois' classic book *When the Lord Speaks to Your Heart* provide much food for thought and meditation for the soul seeking to deepen his or her relationship with the Lord. These uplifting reflections are filled with hope, healing, comfort, encouragement, love, and friendship. The thoughts contained within these pages can be seen as his extended hand reaching out to yours to bring you ever further along the journey of going both higher and deeper. They will inspire your heart to join itself ever more fully with the Lord's heart in living a life of love: his love. I have long kept a copy of this book on my nightstand and I frequently take it with me on retreat. In its use, may it bring you an abundance of grace and blessings.

JAMES R. MATTALIANO, SJ
DIRECTOR OF CAMPION RENEWAL CENTER, WESTON, MA

Preface

Father Gaston Courtois was drawn to a life of intimacy with God. This intimacy grew over the years, and the many tasks this man of action carried out never affected his inclination for profound prayer, one of his most notable characteristics. On the contrary, his interior life, comprised of listening to the Lord, of heart-to-heart talks and face-to-face moments with Jesus, motivated his entire pastoral activity. In the silence of prayer, he received not only ideas that filled his mind, but also the ability and means to carry them out.

For many years, Father Courtois carried notebooks in his pocket in which he wrote as if taking down the Lord's dictation. These notebooks (in addition to Courtois' many other works, most of them unfortunately out of print) contain his more personal interactions with the One who was his all. Father Courtois did not withhold from others what he thought came from God.

When someone would say to him, with a touch of envy, "You are lucky that the Lord speaks to you this way," he would reply that he did not hear any "voice": "I only express in my own words what I think he wants me to say." At times he questioned the authenticity of these notes, as he once testified at the end of a retreat in 1959. Jesus responded to him: "What are you afraid of? An illusion? If my words sound like those in the Gospel, if they help you to be more humble, more obedient, more detached, more generous, more charitable, and more united to me, what have you to fear? My words are *spirit* and *life*. A tree is judged by its fruit. As for you, live in an attitude of conversation with me. This will be the best conclusion of your retreat."

And another time he heard the Lord tell him: "Look at me. Speak to me. Listen to me most lovingly, so that you may become more like me. I will take care of the rest. Haven't you learned that I can cast light in minutes, a light that the most scholarly books cannot cast—or, if they can, is it not because they were prayed over before being written and are the extension or echo of my own word? So, ask me questions. I will reply in my own way when I think best, but you will have an answer—a clear and forceful answer."

Some years later Jesus told him that these intimate conversations might be useful for others as well. "You must grasp the ideas I give you and express them in your own words shortly after I give them to you. Otherwise, they will disappear in the mist of oblivion. If I cause them to well up in your mind, first of all it is for your sake, since they will help you think as I do, see things as I see them, and interpret signs as I want them to be understood in the light and shadow of faith. Then they are for all your brothers and sisters in the world. Each one needs the light I give you, just as you yourself absorb the light I reflect in their words, in their writings, in their conduct. My inspiration will sustain not only your prayers but also your preaching by word or pen—*contemplata aliis tradere*" ("give the fruit of contemplation to others").

Father Courtois' first title for his notebooks was *At the Master's Feet*. In the last notebook, written between 1967 and 1968, he wrote this title on the flyleaf: *When the Lord Speaks to the Heart*. He chose this as the title for his notes to be published, believing it more in keeping with his purpose.

Father Courtois wanted and sought only to love the Lord as much as possible, and to strive with all his might to make him loved. May this posthumous message continue the mission of his entire life.

AGNÈS RICHOMME
BIOGRAPHER OF FATHER GASTON COURTOIS

How to Use This Book

When the Lord Speaks to Your Heart is an English adaptation of the book *Quand le Seigneur parle au coeur*. As explained above, it contains the messages that Father Gaston Courtois received from the Lord Jesus. The thoughts are phrased in such a way that it is evident that Jesus is the one speaking.

In this edition, we have divided the material to cover each day of the year. The thoughts for each day, though short, contain profound material for reflection. To gain the most from it, you may wish to spend a few moments in prayer before reading it, and then reflect on it for a while and conclude with a prayer. If you read them in the morning, the reading can set the tone for your day and help you live it in union with Jesus. If you read a passage in the evening, you can recall it in the morning as you go about your daily work.

You may wish to use this prayer to the Holy Spirit:

Come, Holy Spirit, fill the hearts of your faithful.
And kindle in them the fire of your love.
Send forth your spirit and they shall be created.
And you shall renew the face of the earth.

Let us pray.

O God, you instructed the hearts of the faithful by the light of the Holy Spirit; grant us in the same Spirit to be truly wise, and ever to rejoice in his consolation. Through Christ our Lord. Amen.

JANUARY

I love that you know how to find me, recognize me, and perceive me in your brothers and sisters, in nature, in small or great events. All is grace and I am there. (117)*

---

* The parenthetical citations following each quote refer to the corresponding reference numbers in the French edition.

January 1

Listen. Understand. Ponder. Absorb. Put into practice. I know it is difficult to listen to me when other sounds fill your head. There must be silence, an experience of the desert. You are shocked by the aridity of the void. Yet if you are faithful, if you persevere, then your well-Beloved will make his voice heard. Your heart will burn, and this inner ardor will bring you peace and fruitfulness. Then you will relish just how gracious your Lord is, how light is his burden. You will experience, even beyond the time you devote exclusively to me, the reality of *dilectus meus mihi et ego illi* ("my beloved is mine and I am his," see Song 2:16). *(1)*

January 2

Despite obstacles, feelings of aversion, or temptations to faintheartedness, the more you seek me and desire to listen, the more you will perceive my response. My Spirit will animate you and suggest not only what I ask you to say, but what I propose that you do. Then what you say and do will be fruitful.

My word and the light it casts help everything find its true place within my immense love. *(2–3)*

January 3

Look at me. Speak to me. Listen to me. I am not only the witness to truth but Truth itself. I am not only the way of life but Life itself. I am not only a ray of light but Light itself.

The one who communicates with me communicates with Truth. The one who receives me receives Life. The one who follows me walks along the pathway of light, and my light grows in that person.

Speak to me spontaneously about everything that troubles you. I allow plenty of room for your initiative. Do not think that I am indifferent to what troubles you, for you are mine. It is essential that you be mindful of me, and speak to me with the fullness of love and with all the confidence you can muster. (5–6)

January 4

I speak within the inmost depths of your soul, where your mind is enriched through communion with me. You do not need to immediately discern what I say to you. What is important is to fill your mind with my thoughts. Afterward you will be able to interpret and express them.

Those who never hear me and who regrettably harden their hearts are to be pitied. Ah! If only they would come to me with the soul of a child. "I thank you, Father, Lord of heaven and earth, because you have hidden these things from the wise and the intelligent and have revealed them to infants" (Mt 11:25). If anyone feels thirsty, let him or her come to me and drink. Yes, let all drink the milk of my way of thinking. (7–8)

January 5

Always be on the alert. It is I who can give you the light you so urgently need. My light will fortify your spirit and clarify your thoughts, so that you may find solutions for the problems you face.

I would like to act through you more and more, so never stop directing your will toward me. Strip yourself of yourself. Take upon yourself the attitude of a member of my Body, having only me as your reason for living and the goal of your life.

Call upon me for help—gently, calmly, and lovingly. Do not think I am insensitive to the tenderness of affection. Yes, tell me you love me, but prove it to me even more. *(9–11)*

January 6

Tell me how you spent the day. I know already, of course, but I love hearing it from you, just as a mother loves to hear the chatter of her child coming home from school. Let me know about your desires, your projects, your boredom, your difficulties. Can't I help you overcome them?

Speak to me about my Church, the bishops, your colleagues, the missions, nuns, vocations, the sick, sinners, the poor, and workers. Yes, speak to me especially of this working class that has too many virtues not to be Christian, at least in desire. Is it not among oppressed workers, often crushed by cares and woes, that profound generosity is found? Do they not have a greater tendency to answer "yes" to my appeals? *(12)*

January 7

Speak to me of all those who suffer in their mind, in their flesh, in their heart, and in their dignity. Speak to me of all those

who have died, all those who know they are going to die and are
frightened or peaceful, and all those who are going to die and do
not know when it will happen.

Speak to me of my extension in the world; of what I work out
within the innermost depths of hearts; and of what I also bring
about in heaven to the glory of my Father, of Mary, and of the
blessed. *(13–14)*

January 8

Do you have any questions to ask me? Do not hesitate. I am
the key to all problems. I may not give you the answer right away,
but if your question comes from a loving heart, the response will
come, either through the intervention of the Spirit or through the
events that transpire in your life.

Do you want to tell me what you desire for yourself, for others, for me? Do not be afraid to ask me for a lot. By doing so, you
hasten, in an undeniable yet invisible way, the hour when all
humanity will be assumed into me. You will cause the level of love
to rise and will extend my presence in the hearts of men and
women. *(15–16)*

January 9

I have many ways to make you understand; you will know
only some of them on earth. But in order to perceive these
truths—limited as they may be—you need to encounter me
more. If you made yourself docile, I would speak even more
often. To be docile one must first of all be humble, consider

oneself ready and willing to sit at the Master's feet, and above all be close to his heart where one can comprehend all without need of formulas. It means being attentive to the movements of grace, to the signs of the Holy Spirit, and to the ineffable breath of my thought. *(18)*

January 10

May your life be an endless conversation with me. Nowadays people talk much about dialogue. Why not dialogue with me? Am I not there, at your very center, beholding every movement of your heart, attentive to your thoughts and the orientation of your desires? Speak to me quite simply, paying no attention to how you express yourself. I am much more concerned with what you want to express than with the words you use. *(20)*

January 11

I am the Word. I am the Word who is never silent. If one listens attentively, one perceives my voice through the lowliest as well as the highest things in nature, through the most diverse beings, and through the most ordinary daily circumstances. It is a question of faith, a faith I must ask for your human brothers and sisters who have lost or not yet received it. Above all, it is a question of love. If one lived more for me than for oneself, that person would be attracted by the slightest murmur of my interior voice and would more easily establish a relationship of intimacy with me. *(21)*

January 12

Call upon me as the light that can clarify your mind, the fire that can inflame your heart, the force that can refresh your energies. Call upon me especially as your friend, who desires to share with you all that is your life; as your Savior, who yearns to purify your soul of its egotism; and as your God, who desires to unite you to himself as closely as possible here below, while waiting to embrace you fully in the light of eternity. *(22)*

January 13

Call upon me. Love me. Let yourself be flooded with the conviction of being passionately loved as you are, with all your limitations and miseries, so that you may become what I desire you to be: the living, burning coals of divine charity. Then instinctively you will think of me and others before living for yourself. You will live in divine communion with me and in universal communion with others, identified with me and at the same time with others. You will then allow me to serve as a bond between my Father in heaven and my brothers and sisters on earth. *(23)*

January 14

Speak *to* me before speaking *about* me. Speak to me in all simplicity, most familiarly and with a smile. Those who speak about me without my speaking through them—what can they say about me? So many false ideas circulate about me, even among Christians, and much more among those who do not believe in me.

Keep talking with me after our conversations in the chapel. Think about my presence—with you, in you. Do this while going about what you have to do, and from time to time lovingly lift your eyes toward me.... (19)

January 15

Inner demons must be silenced: the demons of pride, the drive for power, the spirit of domination, aggressiveness, and eroticism, which obscure the mind and harden the heart.

Silence minor occupations, excessive concerns, and sterile lies.

Silence futile distractions, self-seeking, rash judgments.

But this is not enough. You must also desire that my thoughts permeate your spirit and gently impose themselves on your mind. (26–27)

January 16

Above all do not be impatient or struggle. Instead be at peace and ready to keep my word, carrying it out with good intentions. It is the seed of truth, light, and happiness. It is the seed of eternity that transfigures the most lowly things and deeds of the earth.

When my word has been absorbed, savored, and profoundly relished, then its full worth will be understood. A person will then be ready to sacrifice all those seemingly necessary attachments. I carry out my work of peace and love in the Church through prayerful souls who are compliant with my action. (27–28)

January 17

It is helpful to have enough time in which to become more aware of my presence.

First, ask me more earnestly to purge you of all that hinders you from listening to, hearing, pondering, absorbing, and putting my word into practice. Indeed I am he who is speaking to you. But you can only hear me if you listen to me. You can only listen to me if your love is truly unpolluted by self-concern and has the characteristics of a sacrificial love in communion with mine.

Second, be faithful, consecrating to me your innermost being, where I am ever-present, ever-acting, ever-loving.

Third, smile more and more at me. You know I love the person who gives with a smile. Smile at me. Smile at everybody. Smile at everything. A smile contains, much more than you think, the expressive tenderness of true love based on the giving of self. The more you give, the more I give myself to you in return. *(30)*

January 18

You are not only to live face to face *with* the Lord, but *in* your Lord. The more you strive to have no feelings other than mine, the more you will be conscious of this marvelous living together, which through me unites you to the Trinity, to all the saints, and to all the members of my mystical Body. You are never alone. Your life is essentially communitarian. *(31)*

January 19

I stand at the door of your soul and knock. If you hear my voice and open wide the door to me, then I will enter within you and we will dine together (see Rev 3:20). Do not worry about the menu. I bring the greatest part of the banquet, along with joy—my joy, which is to see you relish it so that you may give more of me to your brothers and sisters. Think of them when you think of me. Include them in your prayer, offering yourself and them to me. Carry them with you as you let yourself be immersed in me. (32)

January 20

Think, pray, and act in me. I am with you, and you are with me. I desire this kind of intimacy with you.

Live with me as with a friend you would never abandon. Do not drive me away from your heart or your mind. (32)

January 21

Pay attention to my presence.

You know that I am near you and within you and others. But it is one thing to know that, another to perceive it clearly. Ask me often for this grace. Your humble and persevering prayer will not be refused. It is the most concrete expression of living faith and ardent charity. (32)

January 22

Pay attention to my gaze.

You know that you never leave my sight. If only you could see how I gaze on you, with such love, tenderness, and desire! This gaze, attentive to your innermost choices, ever-benevolent, encouraging, is always ready to sustain and help you! But hear this! You must encounter my loving gaze in faith, desire it in hope, and cherish it in love. (32)

January 23

Pay attention to my love.

You know that I am love, but I am even so much more than you know. Adore and have trust. The surprises I have in store for you will be even more beautiful than you can imagine. The time after death will be that of the victory of my love over all human limitations not deliberately willed as obstacles to it. From now on, ask for the grace of a keener, more intuitive perception of my immense love for you. (32)

January 24

Pay attention to my word.

You know that within you I am the very One who speaks; my word is spirit and life. But what does it serve to expound upon the Father's riches if your heart is not listening intently to accept and assimilate them? You know I speak in the ideas I cause to come to light in your mind. On beginning, you must be faithful to my Spirit. On arrival, you must be intent on receiving the divine pearl. Then your life will be fertile. (32)

January 25

Your life would be simpler and more fruitful if you gave me all the room I yearn for in your mind and heart. You yearn for my coming, my growth, and my taking possession.

First, take into account that you are nothing and can do nothing by yourself to increase by a single degree the intimacy of my presence within you. You must humbly ask it of me in union with our Lady.

Then, in the measure of the grace imparted to you, do not let any occasion go by to unite yourself to me, to vanish within me. Plunge into me confidently, and let me then act through you. (35)

January 26

This statement of mine is not a laughing matter: "I want to feel my life throbbing within you. I want to feel my love burning in your heart." And now I add: "I want to feel my light shining in your mind." But this presupposes the denial of your ego as much as possible.

My gaze at you is true, lucid, and profound. Far from running away from it, seek it. It will help you discover any attachment and self-seeking that remains in you. It will inspire you to forget yourself even more for the sake of others. (36–37)

January 27

You should not be able to do without me, so that I can be with you as much as my heart desires. Yet if human nature is not constantly stimulated, it slackens its effort and becomes distracted. This explains the need for these constant moments of renewing contact with me. As long as you are on earth, nothing is ever over; you must always begin again. But each fresh impulse brings a rebirth and increase of love. (38)

January 28

Desire me. Am I not he who fully responds to the aspirations I myself placed in your heart? I will come to you. I will grow within you. I will work within you, as much as you desire. I am all that is lacking in you, and possessing me makes you sense the vanity of every other desire. Why want anything else save to live as one with me? How futile and disorderly are all desires that do not lead to me! (39)

January 29

Through all your occupations—from the time you rise to the time you retire, from the time you pray to the time you work, from the time you dine to the time you rest—let me feel the intensity of your desire. May you yearn for me; may your heart seek me; with all your being may you wish to be one with me.

Desire me for yourself, for without me you can achieve nothing effective or even useful on the spiritual plane.

Desire me for others. You only communicate me . . . inasmuch as it is I who act through you. *(39)*

January 30

Live in me: you will live through me; you will effectively act for me; and your last years will efficaciously serve my Church.

Dwell in me as in your very own home. Remember, whoever lives in me bears much fruit.

Live in my prayer. Live in the ever-streaming flood of desires, praises, and acts of thanksgiving that surge from my heart.

Live in my will. Unite yourself to my will for you and to all my designs of love.

Live in my wounds; they remain open so long as the world is not completely united to me. Draw from my wounds the power to sacrifice on behalf of your sisters and brothers. Your choices can be decisive for many.

Live in my heart. Let me inflame your heart with the intense fire of love. If only you could be set aglow. *(40–41)*

January 31

Think a bit more often about what pleases me: my dwelling in the souls of children; the purity of their hearts; their sacrifices of love, so generous at times; the simplicity and fullness of their self-giving. I blossom in many children's hearts. Nothing tarnishes the crystal of their souls, and teachers can lead them, guide them, and encourage them to come to me. *(42)*

FEBRUARY

My dream is that under your impulse, through your initiative, and with your intelligent cooperation, by putting to work the gifts and talents I have entrusted to you, human activities and lives may be enriched through the growth of my love in each person. (68)

February 1

The priest, who loyal to the Holy Spirit and to my Mother gradually becomes conscious of my presence and acts accordingly, gives me great joy. I also rejoice in the simple souls who are in every place, in all countries. They are not overcome by pride, are not overly concerned with themselves, and they think of others more than of themselves. In a word, they habitually forget themselves in order to live by serving my love. (43)

February 2

Love me as I want you to love me, and feel it. Love everyone as I want you to love them, and feel it. Detach from yourself. Do not overestimate yourself but make me the center of your life, and feel it.

Never forget me. If only you knew how often I am forgotten, even by my best friends, even by you! Ask me often for the grace not to forget me. You understand clearly the riches to be gained, for yourself and for those who depend on you, from never forgetting me, at least insofar as circumstances permit. (44–45)

February 3

Be mindful of my presence in you, in your neighbor, and in the Host.

Your mindfulness of my presence transfigures all you do: it divinely enlightens your thoughts, your words, your actions, your sacrifices, your sufferings, and your joys.

Do not forget my desires: my Father's glory, the advancement of my kingdom in all hearts, the sanctification of my Church, the fulfillment of my Father's will in you—his eternal dream for you and your place in the holy history of humanity. *(46)*

February 4

I lead you. Be at peace—but do not forget me. I am he who transforms all, who transfigures all, no matter how seldom my help is requested. When you invite me to unite myself to you, all you accomplish or all you suffer has a special value, a divine value. Avail yourself of my help then, for it gives your life the whole dimension of eternity. *(47)*

February 5

At times, you must exert yourself, lest you fall again into your personal problems. I never stop acting within and with you. I take up the discussions and conflicts of life each time you request this of me. Do not think that what I ask of you is so difficult. I want to guide you much more through constant and loving communion with my Divine Presence than through heroically borne sufferings. *(48)*

February 6

Share everything with me. Put me in everything you do. Ask me for help and advice more often. You will double your interior joy, for I am the ever-flowing source of living joy. What a pity it is to represent me as someone austere, inhuman, dour. Communion with my love surpasses all pain and transforms it into tranquil and reassuring joys. *(48)*

February 7

Seek constantly to please me. Let that be the fundamental orientation of your heart and your will. I am much more sensitive than is thought to little things and to loyal attentions.

If you knew how much I love you, you would never be afraid of me. Thrilled, you would cast yourself into my arms. You would live with abandon, trusting in my immense tenderness. Even in the midst of your most absorbing tasks, you would not forget me, and within me you would accomplish everything. *(49–50)*

February 8

To hear my voice, you must put yourself in a frame of mind that makes harmony of thought with me easy.

First, loyally open your soul to me. Loyally—that is, without reservation, with the intense desire to listen to me, with the will to make the sacrifices my Spirit may suggest to you.

Resolutely banish from your mind all that is not me or according to my mind. Remove useless or contrary preoccupations.

Humble yourself. Tell yourself—and you must tell yourself often—that by yourself you are *nothing*; that of yourself you are not capable of any good, any fruitfulness, or any profound and lasting efficacy. *(51)*

February 9

Rekindle within yourself all the love I have made you capable of giving. As a consequence of your external life, the coals tend to die. You must regularly rekindle the fire of your heart. Generously stir in the twigs of your sacrifices; call often upon the Holy Spirit to help you; repeat to me those words of love that will draw me to you and will make your spiritual hearing keener.

Then, in silence, adore me. Sit tranquilly at my feet. Hear me call you by name. *(51)*

February 10

Make all your gifts, desires, and aspirations mine. I alone can fill you without you ever becoming satiated. Regard as lost the time you have not spent loving me. This does not mean that you must always be conscious of my love, but that you should ever wish and deeply desire it.

More and more, in silent and familiar conversations, will you meet with me. Be confident. Each soul has its own personal style of conversation with me. *(52–53)*

February 11

Unite yourself with all the unknown mystics now living on earth. You owe much to them without knowing it. After all, it is they who draw down on humanity my graces of redemption. Intensely desire that truly contemplative souls will multiply in the world.

The important aim of your mission is to contribute from within, to bring about a more intense current of love that will flow through the world. (54)

February 12

Your thoughts, and above all your heart, must be directed instinctively toward me, as the compass is drawn to its magnetic pole. Work and relationships prevent you from thinking explicitly and constantly of me; but if, as soon as you have a free moment, you even blink an eye faithfully at me, gradually these acts of love will influence your activities during the day. Of course I know they are for me—even when you do not say so—yet how much better it is when you do. (55)

February 13

I never leave you alone. Why do you still leave me alone so often, when you could, by a slight effort, seek me—if not find me—within yourself and in others? Think about asking me for the grace to do this. I always grant such a grace when it is loyally and insistently requested of me. Then, repeat often: "I know you are there and I love you." These simple words, pronounced lovingly, will win for you a rekindling of fire. Finally, strive to live with me in your heart: little by little, you will live more with me in the hearts of others. Then you will understand them better and you will help them more. (55)

February 14

Your prayers, activities, and sufferings will bear fruit through intense union with me. I myself—the One who adores, praises, thanks, loves, offers himself to, and prays to the Father—am in you. Join in my adoration, my praise, my act of thanksgiving, my outpourings of love, my redemptive oblation, my immense desires. You will discover your interior prayer flowing in mine. For there is only one prayer that counts: my prayer, which I express in you. . . . (56)

February 15

Adore in spirit and in truth. Only regular contemplation brings about an interiorizing of prayer, faith, and charity, as well as the radiance of my bounty, my humility, and my profound joy.

Contemplation alone enables me to carry out my delicate work in a person; it allows me to tighten my divine embrace and engrave on the soul my deepening imprint. (56)

February 16

Call me. I ask only to come, but tell me more often:

"Come, Jesus, that I may fully carry out everything you expect of me.

"Come, Jesus, that I may help souls as you desire me to, so as to fulfill your plan of love for them.

"Come, Jesus, that I may love you as you want me to love you." (57)

February 17

Develop in yourself, under the influence of my Spirit and of my Mother, the triad of faith, hope, and love. Through these virtues cling to me with all your might, hunger for me with your whole being, and unite yourself to me with all your heart.

You must be so aware of my presence within you that you feel it in your very bones. Do not waste time acting without love. I am the essence of your soul. (59–62)

February 18

My love has harmonies as diverse as they are powerful. To understand them, you must live in constant and profound union with me. Then, in the innermost recesses of your heart singing in unison with mine, the symphony will continue in manifold variations.

Never let intimacy with me tire or bore you. If you feel any fatigue at all, this is because you have lost the rhythm and have not kept in tune with me. By yourself, you sing off-key and are soon exhausted and out of breath. Call me sweetly and with confidence, and the interior melody will come back to you. (63–64)

February 19

No painter can fully depict certain colors, like those at sunset. Similarly, I alone can give certain interior joys. My love is always sufficient; it has a thousand expressions and a thousand new inventions. If only you would profit from this love, for yourself first and then to reveal me to multitudes of other souls.

When you love me deeply, I am begotten within you, which enables you to radiate me invisibly to those who draw near you. (65–66)

February 20

Nothing is more important than the quality of your relationship with me. Your day's work reflects the quality of your relationship with me. Have you been distant and reticent, or fervent, loving, and attentive? I do not stop paying attention to you. How about you? Why do you pay more attention to passing things than to me, who does not pass away? Don't you realize that if you turn to me, I would help you solve the problems of daily life? Don't you know that you can find in me solutions that take everything into account, even unseen data? Don't you think you would save time, and be less tired, if you turned to me more often? It would be an opportunity for me to give myself more, which is, as you well know, the natural inclination of my heart. (66)

February 21

Live of me. Nourish yourself on my thoughts, which are the expression of my Spirit. They are light and life. They also convey power in the measure you embrace them. Nourish yourself on my will. What do I want of you? See, this is what you must do. Act without worrying about where I am leading you. If you make your will one with mine, all within you will serve the glory of my Father and the good of my Church. *(69)*

February 22

Live with me. Am I not your best travel companion? Why do you forget about my presence? Why don't you enter my gaze more often?

Ask me, then, for advice, counsel, and help, and you will see what I give you for treating me as a close friend. The radiance of this familiar and habitual friendship, founded on an ardent spirit of faith, will give your life the stamp that will please me.

Do not waste your time by forgetting me! *Thinking of me multiplies your fruitfulness tenfold. (69)*

February 23

Live for me. If not, for whom will you live besides yourself, that is, for nothing? If only you knew how you deprive yourself and the Church when you do not live *for* me, because to love is, first, to live *for* the sake of being loved.

Act, work, pray, breathe, eat, and relax *for* me. Continually purify your intentions. Loyally do what you can do only for me. Doesn't love demand this? It is a proof of love to expect this from you. You will see that sacrifice rewards, and you will joyously receive a hundredfold of what you are deprived of for me. *(69)*

February 24

Be so bold as to center your life in me and believe that the most effective time you can spend is the time you consecrate exclusively to me. It helps, as you know, to maintain and enrich your interior life while you are active. This makes you sensitive to the signs I send throughout the day and enables you to decipher these signs that I multiply every step along your way. (70)

February 25

A Christian who would make my dream his or her own would find me in everything. That person would hear me, discover me, and go from wonder to wonder by perceiving my ever-living, ever-actual, ever-active, and above all, infinitely loving presence.

Have only loving thoughts in your mind, only rays of goodness in your eyes, only words of love on your lips, only feelings of friendship in your heart, and only wishes of goodness in your will. (71–72)

February 26

So many people imagine that their natural dynamism, their subtle intelligence, and their strength of character will enable them to reach their ends. Poor souls! How great their disappointment or indignation will be over their first failure.

What is important in my eyes is not reading, speaking, or doing many things, but letting me act through you. (222, 328)

February 27

In proportion to the offering of love you bring to the offertory of your Mass, you receive, at the moment of Communion, a fresh infusion of my love. Mass after Mass, it is possible for you to grow in my love, but it is a love that divests, immolates, and gives beyond measure. The only thing that counts, since it is the only thing of value in eternity, is true love. When I look at people, that is what I see right away in each one, that is, this love that does not expect any recompense—or even acknowledgment—this unselfish love that expresses in a personal way what is best in each person. This is the great lesson to be learned from me. *(74)*

February 28

Come to *me* and look at *me*. Looking at *me*, read and learn.

Immerse yourself in my heart and understand. Come near to my will and be inflamed.

I am *flame*; I am *fire*; I am *love*.

It is so simple to love, yet how few, even among the devout, know this secret. True love is only found in forgetting one's self. Too often when we think we love others, we are really only loving ourselves. *(75–77)*

February 29

This is a litany of love I expect from you:

Jesus, my love, I love you.

Jesus, my fire, I love you.

Jesus, my strength, I love you.
Jesus, my light, I love you.
Jesus, my sufficiency, I love you.
Jesus, my host, I love you.
Jesus, my prayer, I love you.
Jesus, my all, I love you. (58)

MARCH

You know very well that of yourself, you are nothing and you can do nothing—but you will be astonished one day when you see what we have done together. (112)

March 1

Avoid complications above all. Summon all the reserves of affection in your heart, which I have placed there, and direct them toward me without further delay.

Put yourself under the influence of the Holy Spirit, who will inflame you always more. If you were truly a burning ember, how many souls you would save. My true union with souls is measured by the warmth of their love for me and for others. *(78–79)*

March 2

You know that I am infinite, passionate, devouring love; or rather, you know it intellectually but not concretely enough. I can only exercise my love toward you in the measure you authorize me to do so. You do this by the genuine disposability of your entire person to the action of my Spirit, through my divine love distributed in hearts. If you knew how consumed God is with the desire to give and be given, to penetrate, to take over, to enrich, to assimilate a loved being, to fit him or her into the Father's design of love, and to absorb, assume, inspire, be concerned about, and identify himself with that person! . . . But there is an absolute condition. It is the *jam non ego* ("no longer I . . ."). Egocentricity, pride, self-love, possessiveness, and subtle seeking of the human ego must be consumed in the fire of love. *(80)*

March 3

Give me quality love. The more humility a soul has, the purer its love; the more spirit of sacrifice, the truer its love; the more communion with the Holy Spirit, the stronger its love.

If you were more intensely passionate about my love, many things would fall into place for you. How many times you let yourself be troubled by clouds of no importance and neglected the realities that really matter. *(81–82)*

March 4

In you, I am he who loves the Father.

Can you imagine the strength and intensity of my love for the Father? He begets me eternally. Mystery of the gift, mystery of the perfect love that is the object of contemplation and the praise of the elect in heaven. In you, I am he who loves the Holy Spirit.

The Holy Spirit, the living bond linking me to the Father, the fundamental kiss of our love; we are distinct Persons yet linked together like fire and flame. *(83)*

March 5

In you, I am he who loves Mary.

With *filial love*—for I am really and truly her child more than any son on earth is the child of its mother.

With *redemptive love* that merited her preservation from original sin and closely associated her to the work of the salvation of the world. *(83)*

March 6

In you, I am he who loves all people now living on earth.

I love all the souls who make up your spiritual children, all those whom I will reveal to you one day as having benefited more directly from your renunciations, from your sufferings, from your labors, as well as all other people, all without exception. (83)

March 7

Only what you infuse with love has any worth in my kingdom and in my eyes. Things are of worth only to their degree of love. Men and women are praiseworthy only to the degree of their loving self-offering. This alone is of value. You must apply all your resources and exert yourself so that you will be permeated by my love. Expending your resources for divine love is a gift that must be asked for constantly and exhaustively. Exerting yourself out of charity is a virtue that requires much courage.

Ah, if only people were willing to rectify their scale of values according to this understanding! If only they could see the importance of love in their life. (84)

March 8

To love is to think of me, to look on me, to listen to me, to unite oneself with me, to share everything with me. Your whole life is a series of uninterrupted choices for or against this love, which predisposes you to renounce yourself for the good of others. The more love grows in a soul, the more it raises the level of humanity. But when a soul says "no" to the offer to share in this love, it fails to advance the divine enrichment of the world and slows the spiritual development of the earth's people. (85)

March 9

The one who makes great efforts to love as my heart loves will see all beings and all things as I see them. That person interiorly understands the divine message I wish to bring him through others.

The more you perceive my love in a living, experiential way, the more you will be able to reveal it to others. This is the kind of testimony I expect from you. (86, 90)

March 10

Have you noticed that the more faithful you are to prayer, the less boring it is? You are only bored by what you neglect. When you persevere in this time of prayer, you obtain the grace to taste and at times relish it—or, in any case, to endure and, if there be cause, to offer up. (87–88)

March 11

Within me, you can surely find the Father and the Holy Spirit—for the Father is in me and I am in the Father, and the Holy Spirit unites us to one another in an ineffable union: the reciprocal coexistence of me, the Son, with the Father and the Holy Spirit. (90)

March 12

Within me, you find my Mother Mary, who is united with me in an incomparable way and through whom I continue to give myself to the world. You find your guardian angel, faithful companion of your earthly life, devoted messenger, and ever-present protector. You also find all the saints of heaven, from the patriarchs down to the apostles, from the prophets down to the martyrs. (90)

March 13

Within me, you find all priests who are united to me by virtue of their priestly ordination, which serves to identify them with him in whose name they speak. You find all Christians, but also all people of good will, no matter who they are. You find the suffering, the sick, the dying, and all the deceased in purgatory who, in my hidden presence, discover the basis for their ardent hope. (90)

March 14

Within me, you find the whole world, known and unknown, all the beauties, all the riches of nature and science that surpass what the most learned persons can even imagine. You find the secret of total, self-giving love, for I am essentially he who loves and who desires to bring fire on earth to set humanity aflame with eternal joy and happiness. (90)

March 15

I always wait for you—not impatiently, knowing how weak and fragile you are, but most eager to listen to you and feel that you are listening to my word. Do not waste your mind thinking about so many ephemeral and useless things. Do not squander the little time you have in so many futilities. Think of my being there—I, your teacher, your friend, your servant—and turn toward me. How much more your radiance would intensify and extend if you paid more and more attention to me! (91)

March 16

Keep this in mind: no matter what activity you carry out, no matter what suffering you endure, the union of love that inspires it makes it worthwhile. Seek to unite yourself to me more and more. Unite yourself to my Father. Unite yourself to my oblation. Unite yourself to my action in the world within the depths of hearts. See how selfishness impedes this union, whether you are aware of it or not. On the contrary, see how powerful this union is in generous souls who give themselves over docilely. (92)

March 17

Unite yourself to me in everything you do, and you will do it better and more easily. Unite yourself to me in order to be receptive, understanding, and open to others, and I will allow something from me to pass to them. If you do not want to live apart from me, unite yourself to me more often and more intensely, and do so whether it's sunny or cloudy. (93)

March 18

When you multiply positive acts of love and desire throughout the day, something of the Father's love for me grows in you. Acts of love enable me to be more wholly present in you; they reveal me through your very flesh. Your love must be active and vigilant. If it falls asleep due to faintheartedness or negligence, my life within you will radiate less brightly. *(94)*

March 19

Your faith and love can be renewed in the knowledge of my love for you and for the world.

First you truly perceive my presence, enveloping you interiorly and exteriorly. Do I not dwell in your inmost being? Isn't it right for me to repeat often to you: "Look at me looking at you. Treat me as if you could see me, and smile at me."

Next you have an intellectual knowledge of the infinite Love, which loved you even to the follies of the crib, the Cross, the Host, and the priesthood. My humility and tenderness make me dependent on you and your cooperative good will.

Finally, you hope for what you cannot yet fully know or perceive: the fire of Trinitarian love, which will incite, inflame, and nourish you in and for eternity, making you share our great joy, in sublime and universal charity. *(95)*

March 20

If you only knew how I love it when you think about me as you go about your daily life, not only to be invoked with formal prayers, but to be your true and close friend whom you can rely on. Am I not he who feels what you are undergoing, who assumes your states of soul, who transforms and makes fruitful your desires, your actions, your words . . . ? Everything that fills your days must be an occasion for you to share all the love of your soul. (96)

March 21

We are together as the branch is to the stalk of the vine, as the member is to the body. Together we pray.

We are together in working, speaking, being kind, loving, offering, suffering, dying, and one day seeing and rejoicing with the Father and our Lady. Consciousness of being together is a guarantee of security, fruitfulness, and joy. . . .

Whoever remains in me and I in him will bear much fruit: visible and invisible. I want my joy to shine out through your soul. (97)

March 22

I myself am within you. He who speaks on your behalf never stops asking for the graces you need to fulfill the plan willed by him in the communion of the mystical Body: the Father's eternal design of love toward you. He offers and gives himself unreservedly to the Father, who sees in the Son's oblation the offering of you and all your brothers and sisters. He offers the blessing and purification of the Spirit to all souls now living on earth. He adores, praises, and thanks the Father, and he desires to be the adoration, praise, and thanksgiving of all humanity. (98)

March 23

My love is delicate. I loved you first, and all that you are I gave you. Out of compassion, I do not often remind you of this. I wait for you to render an account of it, to thank me, and to receive your reward.

My love is tender. I am infinite tenderness. If only you knew the riches of my heart and the immense desire I have to fill you with them! Come to me, my little one. Put your head on my shoulder and you will better understand *quam suavis est Dominus tuus* ("how sweet is your Lord"). (99)

March 24

My love is considerate. Nothing that concerns you escapes me. No feeling of your soul is unknown to me. I make all your desires mine to the extent they are in conformity with my Father's design of love and therefore of real concern to you. I make all your intentions mine and faithfully bless all the souls you entrust to me.

My love is merciful. I know better than you the extenuating circumstances and the reasons for your faults, your errors, your flaws. (99)

March 25

My love is strong; it is strong through my might. My love is strong in order to sustain you, to guide you according to the degree that you appeal to it. Whoever relies on my love can never be deceived.

My love is divinely demanding. You understand this. Since I love you for yourself, I want to be able to give myself to you more fully. I can only do so if you faithfully respond to all my invitations of grace, to all the impulses of my Spirit. *(99)*

March 26

Since I love you for the sake of your brothers and sisters, I want to be able to come to them through you more and more. It is up to you to reflect me, and me to reveal and express myself. But I can only do so if you open up the great doors of your heart—and if you respond generously to my calls.

Increasingly come under my Spirit's influence. At the same time, *trust* in my merciful power and *desire* to call on it in order to help yourself and the Church. *(99, 203)*

March 27

Simplify everything, joyful or sorrowful, with love. How I would like to see you practice each day a quarter of an hour of pure, positive, explicit love. In union with me, do so steadily. Begin with one minute, then two, then three. If you persevere, under the

Spirit's influence, you will soon arrive at fifteen. You will then see how many things will fall into place, and you will have a foretaste of what I reserve for you when your hour comes. In this way, you will gradually enter into my immensity without fear of going beyond your depth, since it is I who will be overtaking you. *(100)*

March 28

You must have a love stronger than your excess of activity, stronger than your concerns, stronger than your suffering. What counts in my sight is not the love you feel but the love you show me.

Frequently during the day repeat little, silent acts of adoration to me who loves you so much and who never leaves you. Frequently ask me to make your desire for me, your inclination toward me, and your joy in me increase. That is a prayer I like to grant—but be patient, and do not try to move ahead of my grace. *(101, 103)*

March 29

My kingdom is built from inside. I need generous souls, engaged in inner combat on behalf of their brothers and sisters. What counts is the fire of love growing in hearts, rather than great exterior actions or excellent organizations that from an institutional point of view may seem remarkable, but are actually empty or quite distant from my living and active presence. *(104)*

March 30

Do not accept monotony in love. Seek love and from me find new ways of expressing it. My ways are never monotonous. Show me more often that it is I whom you desire, and say to me, in your name and on behalf of others: *Maranatha.* Come, Lord Jesus, come.

Believe me. I always answer invitations. *(105)*

March 31

Of course there must be fixed points in the spiritual life that serve as signs and support, not as obstacles or "trees concealing the forest."

Let me lead you as I understand you should be led. Do not worry about the future. What did you lack in the past? You will want for nothing, because I will always be with you. When I live in you, you will never want for anything. My presence and tenderness will always be near you, arousing in you acts of thanksgiving, love, and zeal. Even in the sad and harsh hours of your life until now, I was there beside you, as you well discovered, and the tunnels opened up into light. *(107)*

APRIL

Just as for Mary Magdalene on Easter morn, so my heart never ceases calling you by name and waiting for your response. I very softly pronounce your name and I await your ecce adsum *("here I am"), in testimony to your attention and readiness. (17)*

April 1

Whoever desires to come near me more often and more readily will find fresh energy in the contemplation of my divine presence. I am the Fountain of youth, and in me all true renewal occurs—in souls, in homes, and in all societies. *(108)*

April 2

Contemplative life is not a life of ecstasy. It is a life in which I am someone important, someone to be reckoned with, someone who can be counted on. It is also a life of union with my thought; with all my expressions of love, adoration, praise, and thanks; with my unceasing, redemptive oblation as well as my immense desires, which are proportionate to your immense needs. The entire world depends on this vital union with me, on the outpouring of my grace, divine benefits, and especially the continuous embracing of needy, humble, and generous humanity by my divinity. *(108)*

April 3

Your love must endure throughout life—not that it always takes the same form and appearance, or that it fully knows its object. What is essential in love is not full awareness but the fact of loving: thinking of the other before thinking of oneself, living for the other before living for oneself, losing oneself in the other to the point of forgetting self, with the result that the other person increases while "I" decreases. When one truly loves, one thinks only that he or she loves. One loves, and that is everything. *(108)*

April 4

I want to tell you how much I appreciate the prayer you make each day when you receive Holy Communion: "O Jesus, increase in me the desire for you: the desire to possess you, the desire to be possessed by you, and the desire to live more and more in *persona Christi* ('the person of Christ'). Carry out your labor of love in me. Embrace me more closely within your arms. Stamp me with your divine imprint." *(109)*

April 5

Do not be surprised when your prayer is not answered quickly or in a clear and perceptible manner. Persevere. What you ask for comes gradually. It may require not only much time, but also moments of purification that are fulfilled day after day.

The quality of love that inspires life makes it worthwhile. This love may pass through moments of faintness, yet, if it is loyal, it recovers and transforms all it touches—just as the sun hidden by a cloud continues to shine and bursts out again as brightly as before. Love enlightens; love warms; love penetrates; love heals; love rejoices. *(109)*

April 6

Every human being possesses immense possibilities for love. Under the influence of the Spirit, this love may be sublimated and expressed in marvelous acts of generosity, even of self-sacrifice. Under the influence of selfishness, love may degenerate and give way to the worst excesses of depravity and human degradation. To the extent that through grace one purifies and intensifies one's affective powers, he or she will develop and excel in being assumed by me, for I, as infinite tenderness, can only absorb what is of genuine love in the human heart. *(110)*

April 7

I am, above all, a most tender and close friend, who rejoices in the creativity of those he loves, yet is saddened by their errors, blunders, blindness, ambiguities, and resistance. But I am also a friend who is ever ready to pardon and purge the faults of those who come back to him with love and humility.

I see all the possibilities of good in each one, and I am fully prepared to help them blossom—but I can do nothing without your cooperation. In the measure of your attention to my presence you will experience the power of my divine vitality.

I am Light, but also Love. What is not conceived, accomplished, or realized in union with me is destined to perish. *(111)*

April 8

Seek me, the One who is within you, and place yourself freely and with complete generosity under my divine sway. Even though my presence does not always make itself felt, it is exercised and inspires you, unbeknownst to you. You regret that you do not always have a clear awareness of my presence, but what is important is that I am there and that I hear your professions of love. Give me proofs of it—through acceptance of little sacrifices, through minor sufferings borne in union with mine, through frequent and brief intervals between your tasks and readings—and gradually you will grow in a state of fidelity and readiness for all I ask of you. *(113)*

April 9

Faith is a gift I never refuse to one who asks with perseverance. It is for you the sole regular means, an antenna, for communicating with the beyond.

So long as you are on earth, the climate of the soul is a climate of faith, and of meritorious faith, with the divine mixture of light and shadow enabling you to adhere to me without grasping me fully. That is precisely what I expect of you. Where would your merit be if I appeared such as I am, transfigured before you? The more you exercise your faith in love, the more you will come to perceive my divine presence in obscurity. *(114)*

April 10

"The one who is righteous will live by faith" (Rom 1:17). His riches are those unseen realities that gradually become perceptible. Her food is my presence, my gaze, my help, my demands of love. His ambition is to help bring me to birth in many souls. The just person's society is my mystical Body. Her family is the Trinitarian family from which all begins and ends through *me*, with *me,* and in *me.* Live this program more and more. I call you to this above all. *(115)*

April 11

Ask me faithfully for a profound, luminous, solid, clear, and radiant faith. Ask for faith that is not only an intellectual and voluntary adherence to abstract dogmatic truths, but also a perception of my living presence, my interior word, my loving tenderness, and my unspoken desires. Know that I want to listen to you, but ask of me more earnestly. Let your confidence testify to your love for me. *(115)*

April 12

You do not ask enough, for you do not have enough faith. You do not believe that I will listen to you, that I am attentive to your desires. You do not have enough faith to ask with perseverance—without running away at the first obstacle or getting impatient because I seem to keep silent.

You do not have enough faith to appreciate the importance of the graces you must obtain for yourself and for others, for the Church and for the world. You do not have enough faith to ardently and intensely desire what so many people need today. . . .

Am I truly an integral part in your life? Do you not have enough faith to deprive yourself of useless gratifications when, by your sacrifices, you could bring about so many graces for others? *(116)*

April 13

So long as you are on earth, you are blindfolded. It is by faith alone, under my Spirit's influence, that you can be conscious of my presence, hear my voice, and be aware of my love. Act as if you could see me—handsome, tender, loving as I am, and yet so misunderstood, so isolated and set aside by many people to whom I have given so much and whom I am willing to pardon.

I respect humanity so much! I do not want to mistreat anyone. That is why I am so patient, so mindful and sensitive to the least sign of love or respect shown to me. *(118)*

April 14

Call more often on the Holy Spirit. He alone can purify you, inspire you, enlighten you, inflame you, make you a "mediator," fortify you, and make you fruitful.

It is he who can completely deliver you from a mundane spirit, from superficial spirituality, and from self-concern. He makes you appreciate the true spiritual value of humiliations, suffering, effort, and merit in the synthesis of the redemption.

It is he who assures the meritorious aspect of your existence, its full productivity in service of the Church. He suggests what you must do and inspires in you what to ask for, so that I can act through your activity and pray through your prayer. *(120)*

April 15

It is the Holy Spirit who, in the very course of your activities, purifies you of being self-centered, self-opinionated, self-loving, self-willed. He keeps your life within the range of my love. He prevents you from attributing to yourself the good he does through you.

The Holy Spirit sets your heart on fire and makes it beat in unison with mine. He causes inspirations and ideas to spring up in your mind. Insofar as you are docile to him, he will inspire you with right choices, good behavior, and also the desire to return to solitude.

The Holy Spirit gives you the strength to begin and the courage to continue in spite of obstacles, contradictions, and oppositions. He keeps you peaceful, calm, serene, stable, and secure. *(120)*

April 16

You need the Holy Spirit to make you grow in a filial attitude toward the Father—Abba Father—and in a fraternal attitude toward others. May your prayer be based on mine to attain full efficacy: to will firmly, tenaciously, and strongly. You well know that without him, you are only weakness and infirmity.

You need the Holy Spirit to have the fruitfulness I want for you (without him, you are only dust and sterility); to see all things as I see them, with an accurate view of the value of events in the synthesis of history, and to prepare you for what will be your definitive life, helping you pray, love, and act as if you were already in paradise. *(121)*

April 17

Think about the Holy Spirit's presence within you. He can act and make you perceive his divine reality only if you call on him in union with our Lady.

Call on him, not only for yourself but for others, because he is silenced within many hearts that are bound and paralyzed. . . .

Call on him in the name of all whom you meet. He will come to each one according to each person's receptivity—and step by step he will increase the person's capacity for the Spirit.

Call on him in the name of all the unknown souls I entrust to you and for whom your fidelity may merit priceless graces.

Call on him above all in the name of priests and consecrated souls so that genuine contemplatives may be multiplied in today's world. *(122)*

April 18

Whoever inhales my Spirit exhales the charity of my heart. How much better the world would be, how much more alive and united the Church would be, if the Spirit were more ardently desired and more loyally obeyed!

Ask my Mother to include you in the cenacle of souls, poor and lowly, who under her motherly guidance gain for the Church and the world a more abundant and more effective outpouring of my Spirit of love.

Confidence, my little one. I want my life to grow more and more within you. *(124–126)*

April 19

All you offer me, all you do, all you give me, I receive as Savior—and I receive it in the unity of the Holy Spirit. In turn, I offer it to the Father cleansed of all human ambiguity, enriched by my love, for the benefit of the whole Church and of all humanity. (127)

April 20

If you only knew the power of union and unification that belongs to the Holy Spirit, the Spirit of unity. He acts *suaviter et fortiter* ("sweetly and strongly") in the depths of hearts that place themselves loyally under his influence. Relatively few people call on him nowadays, and that is why so many nations, so many communities, and so many families are divided.

Call on him to make our Trinitarian joy increase in your soul, the ineffable joy that proceeds from the fact that each of our Persons, still remaining fully itself, gives itself unreservedly to the other two. Full joy of the gift, of the exchange, of the ceaseless communion into which we dream that you will freely enter. (128)

April 21

Fire of love that wishes to devour but not destroy you, to transform and transfigure you within itself to such a degree that all you touch bursts into flame.

Fire of light and peace: for I pacify all I conquer, and all that I assume will share in my luminous joy.

Fire of unity, in which I suppress everything that divides and goes against my love. Still stronger must be your desire for my coming, my growth, and your possessing me. You must desire fidelity to sacrifice and humility, and I must be permitted to make use of you to manifest my exquisite bounty.

Under my Spirit's influence, may you become a firebrand of love. *(128)*

April 22

Place yourself under my Spirit's influence. The Holy Spirit works ceaselessly within the depths of each being as well as within each human institution. But the Spirit needs apostles faithful to his inspirations, subject to the hierarchy that represents me and continues my presence among you. You must actively collaborate—making the best use possible of the talents and means I have given you, limited though they are. You must faithfully work in communion with me and in communion with your brothers and sisters. Do all this with serenity. I do not ask you to bear the misery of the world on your shoulders, nor even the crises of my Church—but bear them in your heart, in your prayer, and in your sacrifice. *(129)*

April 23

When the Holy Spirit comes upon a human being, he changes him or her into another person, under divine influence. Desire that the ever more abundant coming of the Holy Spirit within you and in the Church be intensified. You will be astonished at the results it will produce in you and in those in whose name you call upon him. *(131–132)*

April 24

I am he who offers. Unite yourself with my offering to the Father, in a homage of praise full of all human joys: the joys of friendship, of art, of repose, of work accomplished, and above all of intimacy with me and of devotion to my service through the service to your neighbor. *(133)*

April 25

Offer me the myrrh of all human sufferings: of the mind, the body, and the heart, of the dying, the imprisoned, the injured, and the lonely.

Call on me sweetly, calmly, and lovingly to help all who are suffering, and you will add worth to their sorrows by uniting them to mine, obtaining for them the favor of alleviation and consolation.

Offer me the gold of all acts of charity, kindness, goodness, friendliness, and devotion that in one way or another are lavishly poured out upon this earth. I see things with eyes of love, and I watch for human actions that are forgetful of self.

Offer these actions to me, that I may promote them and they may extend my growth in the world. Self-offering is the key that opens up waves of graces for others. *(133)*

April 26

Offer to me those who suffer, who are alone, who are discouraged, who struggle, who fall, who weep, who die, as well as those who do not know me or who have deserted me.

Offer the whole world to me . . . all who are prayerful, all who are tepid, all sinners, all who suffer.

Offer every day of this year to me: all the joyful hours and all the sorrowful hours.

Offer them to me so that I may shine through and grow in many who freely adhere to him who alone can fulfill their profound desires for immortality, for justice, and for the peace that I alone can give. (134)

April 27

Live more and more in the name of others, in union with all. Bring them with you in times of prayer as well as in times of rest. Within and through you, I attract those you bring before my eyes. Ardently desire in their name that I may be their light, their salvation, and their joy. Believe deeply that none of your desires, coming from the depths of your being, are ineffective. My mystical Body is perfected by such desires, multiplied throughout the world. (134)

April 28

Do not offer me only the sufferings of others, so that I might alleviate them. Offer me also all the joys of the earth so that I might purify, intensify, and unite them to mine and to those of the saints in heaven.

Do not offer me only the sins of the world, so that I might pardon them as if they had never been committed. Offer me also all the acts of virtue, all the choices carried out for me or for others so that I might weigh them for eternity. (135)

April 29

From now on, offer me also everything good on earth: the purity of little ones, the courage of young people, the beautiful modesty of young girls, the devotion of mothers, the courage of fathers, the goodness of the elderly, the patience of the sick, the sacrifice of those who suffer, and all the acts of love that blossom in human hearts. (135)

April 30

Many of your brothers and sisters have greater goodness than they realize, and are more excellent than they think they are. But I, who see into the depths of each one and who judge all with goodness and tenderness, often discover nuggets of gold under heaps of ashes. It is up to you to offer them to me, so that I may be able to give them worth. Thus by your sacrificial gesture, love will grow in the hearts of all people and finally vanquish hate. (136)

MAY

When you unite yourself to me in your sufferings and in all you do, you place yourself at the very core of abundant spiritual benefits. You obtain all the needed graces of courage and patience. (292)

May 1

Do not give up living, acting, and suffering for others, known or unknown. You do not see here below what you are doing, but I can assure you that nothing is lost that has been joined, by way of modest contribution, to my own prayer, my own sacrifice, my own act of thanksgiving. In this way you enable many unknown souls to draw near to me. . . . Before this vast and anonymous multitude, which would discourage the most zealous wills without the support of my grace, I give you the means to effectively cooperate with me for their spiritual good. Leave it to me. It is I who determines for each person the manner of collaboration I expect. *(136)*

May 2

Be an increasingly faithful subject, pouring out to me all your prayers, activities, acts of kindness, joys and woes, sufferings and human agonies, so that I may assume and purify them and they may thus give life to the world.

Fortunately the world today has generous souls; many others would join them if they were sustained and encouraged. Then they would help others come to me, acknowledge me, and hear me. My appeals would be listened to more, and many, on turning toward me in their inmost hearts, would find their salvation and blossom upon finding me. *(137)*

May 3

Let less time be spent in fruitless gatherings, and come to me more often.

I am the essential Oblation. I give myself wholly to my Father and the Father gives himself wholly to me. At the same time I am he who gives himself and who receives the Holy Spirit in an outburst of love. I want to include all people in this immense and joyous offertory. If I have chosen you, it is precisely so that you may take part in my oblation and contribute to it by bringing many of your brothers and sisters with you. *(137)*

May 4

Come to me and be at peace before me. Even if you do not understand my ideas, my radiance reaches and penetrates you. It will influence your whole life, and that is what is essential.

Come to me, but do not come alone. Think of the masses of people whom I have so greatly pitied, because I could distinguish in each one the things that affect them: distress, concerns, and deepest needs. I am interested in each one of them, but I do not want to do anything for them without the collaboration of those whom I have specially consecrated for their service. *(137)*

May 5

The task is immense. The harvest is abundant. But the workers—the true, faithful, and wise workers who place my kingdom and my holiness above their own concerns—are too few. Let your prayer to the Father, Master of the harvest, be joined more fixedly to mine. Then you will see the number of contemplative apostles and spiritual teachers multiply. Everywhere I inspire the same request in generous souls, in communities, and in the world.

Certainly those who understand and respond are few, but the quality of their appeals compensates for their small numbers. It is essential that they pray and closely unite themselves to the prayer I myself make within them. *(137)*

May 6

Consider yourself part of me, attached by every fiber of your faith and heart, by every orientation of your will. Act as one of my members, knowing your personal limitations, your inability to do anything good by yourself. Pray as one of my members, uniting yourself to the prayer I myself make within you, and unite yourself to the prayer of all humanity. Offer yourself as one of my members, not forgetting that I am always, through love, a sacrificial offering to my Father and that I am longing to unite many now living on earth in this act of homage. As one of my members, receive my Father to whom I give myself and who always gives himself to me in the unity of the Holy Spirit. To the measure you are one with me, you share in the divine riches. Strive to love all whom I love with the same love I have for them. *(138)*

May 7

What is important is not ostentation, being in the spotlight, or fame, but loyal and generous union with me.

What would you think of a ray that cuts itself off from the sun, of a river that deviates from its source, of a flame that separates itself from the fire?

Work for me. You are my servant. Even more than that, you are one of my members, but in reality you work much more for yourself than you do for me. Nothing that is done for me is wasted. *(139–141)*

May 8

Everything shares in my eternal thought. You cannot receive it entirely, for it is infinite, but participation in it will give you some illumination to light your path here below. The concept I have about people and events, my divine thoughts full of love and concern, will help you appreciate others with respect and esteem. Remember that one day you will assign to persons and things of the earth a value quite different from what you assign them now.

My mystical Body grows through love. With love I take up each human soul and divinely transfigure it until it becomes pure charity. Work to infuse more charity in people's hearts through your example, your word, and your writings. This must be the continuous objective of your prayers, sacrifices, and activities. *(142–143)*

May 9

I direct everything in your life, but I must have your active cooperation to help you do freely what my Father wishes. I direct everything in the world, but I patiently wait for men and women to freely agree to work under the conscious or unconscious influence of my Spirit, in order to effectively carry out the Father's designs.

I wait for the world to come to me freely, not only physically but morally, to be willing to join me, to unite its distress to what I suffered in its name at Gethsemane.

I wait for the world to unite sufferings inseparable from the human condition to those I endured in its name during my earthly sojourn and above all during my Passion.

I wait for the world. (144–145)

May 10

What is it that prevents the world from coming to me and immediately listening to my voice calling softly and tirelessly? It is sin. Like sticky tar, sin clogs all the world's spiritual ways, obscures the world's view of the things of heaven, and hinders its movements and slows down its progress. Sin is superficiality, inattentiveness, lack of reflection; the whirlwind of life, of occupations, of news, of relationships. It is the lack of love; and still, the world thirsts for my voice. The word is ever on its lips, but too often its love is only sensuality and self-love. (145)

May 11

I wait for the world: to heal it, purify it, cleanse it, and reestablish in it a true understanding of values. But I need assistants, and that is why I need you. Yes, I need contemplatives who will help me wipe away faults by uniting their life of prayer, work, and love to mine, joining my redemptive oblation through the generous offering of their valuable sufferings. I need contemplatives who unite to my prayer their appeals for missionaries, and spiritual teachers who are filled with my Spirit and for whom the world unconsciously thirsts. (145)

May 12

To become holy you must have courage—for I need your cooperation—and humility, for without me you can do nothing.

I am the river that purifies, sanctifies, and, flowing into the Trinitarian ocean, brings to the divine the best in human beings regenerated by love. If rills, brooks, and streams do not flow into the river, they are lost in the sands or stagnate in the marshes. . . . You must cast into me all you do and all you are. You must also bring to me all your brothers and sisters. Bring their sins that I may pardon them, their joys that I may purify them, and their prayers that I may hear them. Bring their labors that I may confer on them the value of homage due my Father, and their sufferings that I may grant them redemptive power. (147)

May 13

In this vast multitude of humanity I distinguish everyone by name and call each person with all my love. Here, I labor and I act, awaiting the least response to my grace. In the case of some, my grace is fertile and makes my presence more widely felt. They live in my friendship and testify to my existence and my love among their brothers and sisters. In the case of others, the majority, I must wait a long time for them to give me any indication of consent. Yet my mercy is inexhaustible, and where I find the slightest sign of goodness and humility, I act in that person. (148)

May 14

I am pleased that you are not worried about the current disturbances in my Church. Some disturbances are like the wake of a ship, while others occur in the ocean depths. These work in the silence of consciences, mulling over the mitigating circumstances that become an excuse for conflict.

Sow optimism all about you. Of course I ask you to work, to spread my light by word, writing, and especially by the testimony of a life that expresses the good tidings of a God of love, who gathers all people in himself in order to take them up—to the extent they freely consent—into an eternal life of happiness and joy. But above all and beyond all: confidence. I am always there, the eternal Victor. (148)

May 15

This world is passing away . . . while we await a new heaven and earth. Of course, even though the world is ephemeral, it has value, for in the world I willed you and chose you. But while serving to sanctify the world, you must not let it ensnare you. You have a mission—that of helping the world to realize the design of love my Father had in creating it. Although this design is at times mysterious, one day you will see how marvelous it is.

Many colleagues and friends of yours have entered into eternal life. If you could see the pitying yet indulgent look with which they regard what so many hold dear! Too often transitory deceptions hide lasting realities—the only ones that count—from people's eyes. *(150)*

May 16

The world suffers terribly from a lack of spiritual training, and this is largely because there are so few guides. Only the one who humbly appeals to my light and vigilantly contemplates my mysteries—whose life my Gospel permeates—can be a true spiritual guide.

I need apostles who are contemplatives and witnesses more than I need sociologists or armchair theologians who do not pray over their theology and do not live according to what they teach. *(150)*

May 17

Today out of pride too many people, too many priests, think they are authorized to reform my Church. Instead they should begin by reforming themselves and humbly forming around them faithful disciples who will not listen to what they think, but to what I myself think.

You have heard, and can verify, that humanity is currently undergoing a crisis of folly, agitated in every way, without any spiritual realization that would help it regain inspiration in me and stabilize itself.

Alone, the few contemplative souls in the world can put a stop to this profound imbalance that leads to catastrophe. . . . How much time is this going to take? That depends on the availability of the souls I have chosen. *(150)*

May 18

I have conquered the world, evil, sin, and hell, but for my victory to be acknowledged, humanity must freely accept the salvation I offer it.

As long as you are on earth, you can supplicate God in the name of those who do not think of salvation; you can grow in my friendship in the name of and in reparation for those who reject me and turn away from me; you can offer physical and moral sufferings in union with mine in the name of those who undergo them unwillingly.

Nothing that you enable me to take on out of love becomes useless. You may not know how this comes about, but be sure that this offering bears fruit. *(151–152)*

May 19

Bring to me all of humanity's efforts and steps, even hesitant ones. Unite to me their prayers, even those unformulated; their actions, even those uncertain; their acts of kindness, even the imperfect; their various joys; their sufferings, somewhat accepted; their agonies, of which they are more or less aware; and especially their deaths—join all to mine. Together, we will attract more people to him alone who can give them the secret of peace and true happiness. *(153)*

May 20

Many are surprised at the simplicity of my ways and the strength of my divine tenderness.

Nothing is skimpy, nothing is small when it is toiled over or suffered in union with me, I who draw all men and women to myself. The universal dimension is essential for every Christian, even more so for every priest. Beyond you, I see all the souls I have linked to yours. I see their miseries and how much they need my help through you. Everything happens in the synthesis of the divine design, which always draws good from evil and makes love spring up. This happens even where human malice, if not stupidity, seems to put obstacles in the way. *(153–154)*

May 21

The Christian world is overagitated; it is too inclined toward what is external. . . . However, to the extent that there is acceptance of me, desire for me, and the effort to open everything to my love, Christian apostolic life will be filled with joy and fruitfulness.

I alone can bring about the good that lasts. I need servants and instruments who are channels of graces. *(154)*

May 22

I want to make my faithful ones creative, but with me and according to my Father's design. May they never forget that I call them to cooperate with me, and that of themselves they are merely servants. Their life will be fruitful to the degree they dwell in me and permit me to act in them.

Each person has his or her own way of life. If one is faithful, relaxed, and serene, we will travel together. And if a person invites me to stay with him or her, one will see me in the most ordinary details of life. One's heart will burn with love for my Father and for all people. *(154–155)*

May 23

Gather suffering humanity to yourself, and cast all the miseries of the world upon me. Thus you will enable me to use suffering to open wide tightly sealed hearts. I have all the means for assuming, entering into, and healing them, but I want to work with your cooperation. I need cooperation of word, of work, and of witness, but I have greatest need of silent union with me, in joy as well as in suffering. Fill yourself with me to the point that everyone around you will not have the slightest doubt that I am within you, and they will benefit from my divine influence working through you. *(156)*

May 24

Many more possibilities exist for doing good among the young than is thought. They need to be listened to and taken seriously.

How much their education lacks! But most of them ask questions, want to reflect, and are happy to be understood.

Think of these millions of twenty-year-old youths who will make up the world of tomorrow and who seek me more or less consciously. Offer them up often to the action of the Holy Spirit. Even if they do not know him very well, his luminous and gentle activity will penetrate and direct them to build a more fraternal world, instead of foolishly wanting to demolish everything. *(156)*

May 25

The time for creating, organizing, and achieving things is over for you. But I have a hidden mission for you that will benefit and encourage the young. This interior mission is to serve as a bond of union between me and them, to obtain for them the gifts required for a truly efficacious apostolate. Take them all indiscriminately—those of every age, condition, and race—and joyfully offer them up to the radiation of my humility and my Eucharistic silence. *(157)*

May 26

Gentleness and humility go hand in hand; without these two virtues the soul becomes hardened. What good is it to become a star, to gain publicity, applause, and compliments, if one loses the secret to exercising valuable influence in the service of the world and of the Church?

Nothing is more subtle than the poison of pride in a priest's soul. You yourself have often experienced it. Take your brethren upon yourself, especially those for whom apparent and momentary successes risk turning their heads.

If only people would think more about me instead of thinking about themselves! This is why the contemplative life, faithfully lived, brings security and a precious equilibrium. *(158)*

May 27

If I agree to let you share in my suffering, it is to enable you to work effectively for the conversion, purification, and sanctification of many souls united to yours. I need you, and it is normal that by sharing in this work you also share in my redemptive passion. These are the most fruitful hours of your existence. The years go by swiftly. What will remain of your life is the love with which you have suffered and offered yourself. *(160)*

May 28

On earth nothing bears fruit without sorrow humbly accepted and patiently borne, when united with me suffering it within you, feeling it in you, and undergoing it through you.

Pray, suffer, and offer to spend your life in my life; in this way you enable my life of love to be spent in your life. *(160)*

May 29

Suffer along with my suffering. It includes not only the indescribable sufferings of my time on earth and especially of my passion, but all the sorrows I feel and take on in all the members of my mystical Body.

Thanks to this oblation, humanity is purified and sanctified. Enter into the drama of my love, sharing within yourself my redemptive sufferings. *(160)*

May 30

The three dear Apostles I had carefully picked, who had been witnesses of my glory on Tabor, slept while I sweat blood in Gethsemane.

Spiritual fruitfulness cannot be judged according to human criteria.

I want your love to be stronger than your suffering. I want your love for me, which I need so much, to enable my love to be powerful. I want to carry out my salvific action for others through your love for your neighbor. *(160)*

May 31

If you love passionately, your suffering will seem more bearable and you will thank me. You help me more than you realize, but the more you do so out of love of suffering, the suffering I ask of you, the more it will be I who will suffer in you. Those who suffer united to me are the greatest missionaries in the world.

If you saw the world from within as I see it, you would realize the need to find persons of good will here below, in whom I could continue to suffer and die in order to sanctify and vitalize humanity.

In the face of the great selfishness, luxury, and pride that blind many to my grace, witness no longer suffices. The cross is needed. (161–164)

JUNE

The time you spend exposing your soul to the divine radiation of the Host is more beneficial for you than the tasks you feverishly persist in, apart from me. (33)

81

June 1

In order to be able to make a sacrifice when the occasion arises during the day, do not dwell on what you are being deprived of. Instead, gaze at me, and seek the strength that I am ready to grant you through my Spirit.

Feeling my presence and my peace is not necessary. That is why, at times, I permit spiritual trial and painful dryness, a state of purification and merit. A sensitive awareness of my presence, my bounty, and my love is a priceless gift that should not to be taken for granted. That is why you have the right to desire and ask me for it. Do not think you are stronger than you are. Without this gift, would you have the courage to hold on for so long a time? (165)

June 2

Come to me with confidence. I know better than you what is within you, since I dwell there and you belong to me. Call on me for help. I will support you, and you will learn to support others.

Be faithful in offering me voluntary sacrifices . . . to the glory of the three Divine Persons. It is not much, but no matter how small the offering is, it will be extremely precious to me if you are faithful to it, and you will receive greater help through my grace in times of more acute suffering. (166–167)

June 3

When you suffer, let your first reaction be to unite yourself to me who feels within you the pain you feel. Let your second reaction be to offer it up with all the love of which you feel capable, joining it to my ceaseless oblation. Then, do not think too much about yourself. Think about me, who never ceases to take on, until the end of time, the sufferings of men and women on earth.

When you feel poor and inconsequential, come to me even more. Perhaps you won't have fine ideas, but my Spirit will take over within you, and what you absorb unconsciously will rise at just the right moment for the greatest good of many people. *(168)*

June 4

Tell me again and again, with all the fervor you can muster, that you desire to make me loved.

Tell me again and again of your desire to be possessed by me and to live only for me, in the service of your brothers and sisters.

Be generous in this "quest," for it presupposes a minimum of self-denial. It may be said that without self-denial contemplative life is impossible, and without contemplation, authentic and fruitful pastoral life is impossible. *(169)*

June 5

At times my ways are disconcerting. I know this, but they transcend human logic. In humble submission to my guidance you will find more and more peace and, in addition, mysterious fruitfulness will be granted to you.

To be reduced, put aside, unused, when I wish it, does not mean to be useless; rather, the contrary is true. I never work as much as when my servant does not see what I do through him or her. *(169)*

June 6

Think as much as you can of all the human sufferings currently experienced all over the earth. Most people who undergo them do not grasp their meaning; they do not understand the treasure of purification, redemption, and spiritual growth these sufferings represent. Relatively few people have received the grace of understanding the salvific power of pain, when it flows within mine.

Through all the suffering on earth, I am in agony until the end of the world. But never let my apostles disregard any human offering that would enable my divine oblation to bring down, on behalf of humanity, the shower of spiritual benefits it so greatly needs. *(170)*

June 7

Am I not the one who sustains you, always reminding you of this trilogy: *"I appropriate . . . I join . . . I merit . . ."*?

Yes, I take up all human sufferings—all sleeplessness, all agonies, all deaths—and I unite them to mine. Then, following the principle of convergence, I unite them to the great purifying and divinizing river that I am for the world. Be fully convinced that by the very fact of your union with me you win countless spiritual benefits for many unknown brothers and sisters.

How many unknown souls are pacified, consoled, and comforted in this way. How many minds are opened to my light, and hearts opened to my flame, souls who will never doubt where this increase of grace comes from. (172)

June 8

The spirit of atonement forms an integral part of the priestly spirit, and the priest who does not understand this will have an imperfect priesthood. Rebelling at the first ordeal, he will go from frustration to bitterness and will forget the treasure I placed in his hands. Only sacrifice is worthwhile. Without it, the most generous activity becomes fruitless. Of course, every day is not Gethsemane or Calvary, but the priest worthy of this name should know he will encounter both, at certain moments of his existence, in a manner fitted to his capabilities. These moments are the most precious and the most fruitful. (172)

June 9

It is not by lovely feelings that the world is saved, but by communion with me and with my redemptive sacrifice.

One's final years—in which old age, with its caravan of illnesses, restricts a person the most—are the most fruitful for the service of the Church and the world. Accept this and teach those around you that one's declining years possess the secret of an unsuspected spiritual strength. (173)

June 10

If the elderly truly understood their strength and the merits they gain by the least sacrifices made for their brothers and sisters in the world and beyond, they would better grasp the value of their final years. In peace and serenity they would obtain so many graces, while simultaneously gaining for themselves an abundance of light and eternal joys. (386)

June 11

One who suffers with me wins at every turn. Whoever suffers alone is to be pitied. That is why I have often asked you to link all human sufferings and unite them to mine so that they can be valuable and potent. The best way to receive comfort is through this unification.

Far from closing your heart and confining yourself within, suffering should open your heart to all those you encounter and to those who may be suffering miseries you are not even aware of. By this commitment and offering, you most surely carry out your office as priest. In this, there is no potential ambiguity, no possibility of self-seeking, but full availability to my Father's wisdom. (174–175)

June 12

If prayer is the breath of the soul, suffocation is the sign of failure to call for the divine oxygen drawn from me.

You have often found yourself on the cross, but you were able to observe that despite the large and small inconveniences resulting from it, I was always present with you. The cross has allowed you to achieve in your flesh what is lacking to my passion through my Body which is the Church. You have not suffered beyond what is bearable, and if you feel, especially at certain moments, somewhat small, I provide within you what is lacking: many things arrange themselves better than if you took care of them yourself. (175)

June 13

Forget yourself. Renounce yourself. Take greater interest in me, and everything around you will assume its proper place. What counts is the progress, the ascent, of my people. . . . Let me conduct my great undertaking as I understand it. I need your humility more than your external activity. I will use you as I see fit. You are not to ask me for an account of myself; I have no account to give you. Be docile. Be available. Be entirely at my mercy, on the *watch* for my will. I will show you gradually what I expect from you. You will not immediately see what your humility serves. . . . You will feel me more strongly within you . . . , and I will let my light and grace flow through you. (176)

June 14

Almost all human difficulties come from pride. Ask me for the grace of detachment from all vanity, and you will feel more free to come to me and fill yourself with me. What is not me is nothing. Worldly honors hide my presence, because many of those invested in such things are their prisoners. *(177)*

June 15

I love it when you feel you are of "little importance," when you feel feeble and bowed down. Do not be afraid of anything; I am your remedy, your support, and your strength. You are in my hands. I know where I am bringing you.

I lead you through humiliation. Accept it with love and trust; it is the greatest gift I could give you. Even and especially if it is bitter, humiliation offers so many opportunities for spiritual fruitfulness that if you saw things as I do, you would not want to be humiliated less. If you only knew what your humiliations united to mine achieve! The great work of love is carried out through suffering, humiliation, and acts of charity. All else is illusory! How much time is lost, how much pain wasted, how many labors entirely futile, when poisoned by the worm of pride or vanity. *(178–179)*

June 16

The more you see me working through you and helping others to receive well what I inspire you to tell them, the more your influence will be enriched and the less self-opinionated you will be. You will think: "This was not the fruit of my own personal effort. Jesus was in me. He is the one to whom the good outcome and glory is due." *(180)*

June 17

Do not be disturbed when your faculties—your memory, for instance—slow down. I do not judge people's worth by these things. My love makes up for human deficiencies, even failings. Age imposes these limitations on human nature, and they help you to understand how uncertain life can be.

It is good for you to hold yourself lightly, realizing that of yourself you are nothing and have no right to anything. Joyously use the little you have, grateful for the means still available to you. Nothing essential to carrying out the mission I entrust to you will be taken away. But you will begin to exercise your mission in a much purer way, since you will be more aware of the absolute gratuity and relative precariousness of the gifts placed at your disposal. *(181)*

June 18

Be meek. You will encounter many occasions to assert your rights, but divine logic is not human logic. Meekness and patience are begotten of true love, which always excuses and readjusts itself for the sake of true justice.

Be in communion with my meekness. My kindness is not a pretense. My Spirit is at the same time balm and strength, goodness and plenitude of power. Recall these words: "Blessed are the meek, for they will inherit the earth" (Mt 5:5). They will always be in possession of themselves. Even better, they already possess me and will more easily reveal me to others. *(183–184)*

June 19

My degree of radiance in a soul depends on how intimately I am present. But I am always there insofar as I find in the heart of a person my meekness and my humility. In the measure with which you renounce all superiority, you enable me to grow within you. This, as you know, is the secret of all true spiritual fruitfulness in the domain of the unseen. Ask me to be as humble as I want you to be, without pretense but with utter simplicity. *(185)*

June 20

Humility facilitates a person's encounter with God and sheds fresh clarity on all life's daily problems. I truly become the center of your life at such a moment. You act, you write, you speak, and you pray for me. It is no longer you who live, it is I who live within you. I become your *all*, and you find me in all those with whom you come in contact. Your welcome is then more compassionate; your word is more the bearer of my thought; your writings are much more the faithful expression of my mind. Yet for this to happen, how much you must detach yourself from your ego! *(186)*

June 21

May your humility be loyal, trusting, and constant. Ask me for this grace. The more humble you are, the more you will have access to my Light to spread it around you.

Though you do not yet share the fullness of the eternal joy that will be yours, you can, increasingly from now on, cause its reflections to spring up in your soul and shine from within you.

Be more and more a servant of my kindness, my humility, and my joy. (187)

June 22

I need your humiliations much more than your successes. I need your renouncements much more than your enjoyments. How can you pride yourself on what does not belong to you? Like the talents in the Gospel story, all you are and all you have are only loaned to you. Your very cooperation, so precious in my eyes, is only the fruit of my grace. When I reward your merits, they are in truth only my gifts that I crown. You have nothing of your own except your sins, your resistance, and your ambiguities, which my inexhaustible mercy sponges away. (188)

June 23

Leave everything to me. You will always have the light and help you need, and you will have so much more of it the closer you bring your will to mine. Do not be afraid. In due time, I will inspire you with my heart's solutions, and I will even grant you the temporal means to realize them. Do you not find it good to work together? (189)

June 24

You still have a lot of work to do for me, but I will be your inspiration, your support, your light, and your joy. Have only one wish: that I may use you as I see fit, without having to render an account to you or explain why. This is the Father's secret and Our design of love. Do not worry about contradiction, opposition, misunderstandings, calumny, obscurities, or incertitude. Such things come and go, but all this serves to strengthen your faith and provide opportunities to make my redemption more fruitful for the benefit of your innumerable spiritual children. *(190)*

June 25

I am here and I will not abandon you, primarily because I am Love. If only you knew to what extent you are loved! I use you much more than you think. When you feel weak, you are strong with my force, powerful with my power.

Do not rely on yourself; rely on me. Do not rely on your prayer; rely on my prayer, the only prayer of worth. Unite yourself to it. Do not rely on your action or influence; rely on mine. *(192)*

June 26

Do not be afraid. Trust in me. Be concerned about what concerns me. When you are weak, poor, in darkness, in agony, on the cross . . . offer my essential, unceasing, universal offering. Unite your prayer to my prayer. Pray with my prayer. Unite your work to my works; your joys to my joy; your pains, tears, and sufferings to mine. Unite your death with my death.

At present many things are a mystery to you—things that will later become a light and motivation for thanksgiving. In the obscurity of faith, decisions are made in my favor. I myself will be the eternal reward.

Desire that the whole world love me. Your acts of desire are of inestimable value. (192)

June 27

The years remaining for you on earth will be fruitful. This time is like autumn, the season of fruits and beautifully colored leaves about to fall. It is the splendor of the setting sun before it disappears beneath the horizon. As for you, you will gradually disappear in me. You will sink deeper and deeper into the ocean of my love, in which you will find your eternal place. You will be bathed in my light and in my life of glory. (193)

June 28

Be increasingly available; be confident. I have brought you along decidedly difficult roads but I have never abandoned you, and I am at your service in my own way for achieving the grand and beautiful design of love that we have fashioned from all eternity.

I told you that you would suffer a lot—but that I would be near you, within you—and that, sustained by my grace, you would never suffer beyond your strength. (194, 171)

June 29

Believe fully that I am meekness and kindness itself—which in no way prevents me from being just—for I see things in depth and exactly as they are. I can measure better than anyone the degree of your efforts, no matter how slight. That is why I am equally meek and humble of heart, full of tenderness and mercy.

Ah, may no one fear me. Preach trust and hope, and you will reap fresh bursts of generosity in hearts. Excessive fear saddens and diminishes; trustful joy opens up and enlarges. *(195)*

June 30

Ask with faith, with force, and even with confident insistence. If you are not heard in the way you had expected to be, you will soon realize it was because you did not see things as I see them.

Ask for yourself, but also for others. Include in your fervent petitions the immensity of human distress. Take others along with you and present them before me.

Ask for the Church, for the missions, for vocations.

Ask for those who have everything and for those who have nothing, for those who do everything (or think they do everything) and for those who do nothing (or think they do nothing). *(196)*

JULY

The important thing is not to do a lot but to do it well.
To do this requires great love. (146)

July 1

Pray for those who are proud of their strength, their youth, and their talents, and for those who feel insignificant or useless.

Pray for those who are in good health—who take for granted the privilege of having a body and mind in good condition—and for the ill, the feeble, the elderly, the poor. Pray for those who obsess over what happened in the past.

Pray especially for all those who have died or are going to die. *(196)*

July 2

After each storm, silence comes again. Am I not he who stills the roaring waves when I am begged to do so? Therefore, always and above all, have trust in me. When you suffer, remember that I suffer with you, feeling within myself what you are undergoing. At that very moment I always send you my Spirit. If you welcome him, he will help you by flooding you with love during your trial, and you will obtain maximum redemptive value from this cross. So, once more, have confidence. I am within you, weaving the threads of your eternal life, arranging them according to the Father's designs, along with all those of your brothers and sisters now living on earth. The tapestry will only be revealed in its full beauty when it is displayed in heaven. *(197)*

July 3

Trust is the form of love that honors and touches me the most. Nothing hurts me as much as sensing distrust in a heart that wants to love me.

Now, do not be so picky about your conscience. You risk chafing it. Humbly ask my Spirit to enlighten you and help you clear away every vapor that poisons you. Do you not know with certainty that I love you? Should that not be enough for you?

I want you to serve me joyously. The servant's joy honors the Master, and the friend's joy honors the great Friend. *(198–201)*

July 4

At every moment, I have favors for you. You are only occasionally aware of them, but my affection for you is constant. You would be astonished if you could see all that I do for you. Even when suffering, you have nothing to fear. I am always there, and my grace sustains you to make your suffering bear fruit for your brothers and sisters. Then I shower blessings on you throughout the day; I place safeguards around you; I cause ideas to arise in your mind; I inspire feelings of kindness in you; I spread sympathy and confidence around you; and I do many other things you cannot even imagine. *(202)*

July 5

Because you do not tell me enough that you trust in my mercy and tenderness for you, you do not obtain more. Trust that is not asserted is weakened and vanishes.

You are right when you object to the pessimism prevalent today. History shows to what extent I can bring good out of evil. Do not judge by appearances. My Spirit acts unseen within the depths of hearts. It is often during great trials and catastrophes that my word is carried out and my interior kingdom extended. Yes, nothing happens that prohibits me from sustaining you and bringing good out of the situation for my people. *(204)*

July 6

Give yourself trustingly to me. Do not try to understand where I bring you. *Stay close to me* and go forward without hesitating, with your eyes closed and your whole self given over to me.

Stand with confidence behind my vicar, the successor of Saint Peter. I will never reproach you for endeavoring to live and think as one with him, for behind him I am there, teaching what humanity can understand at the present time.

Nothing is more dangerous than to cut yourself off from the hierarchy, even interiorly. Gradually the mind is obscured and the heart hardened, culminating in self-conceit, pride, and catastrophe. *(205–206)*

July 7

Trust in me more and more. I am your light, your might, your power. Without me, you would be darkness, weakness, and sterility. With me, you can overcome any difficulty. But do not boast or take pride in this, for that would be attributing to yourself what is not yours. Act more often in dependence on me.

Trust me. If at times I need your suffering to make up for human ambiguities and resistances, do not forget that, sustained by my grace, you will never be tried beyond your strength. "For my yoke is easy, and my burden is light" (Mt 11:30). For love of you and the world, I associate you with my redemption. Above all, I am tenderness, delicacy, and kindness. *(207–208)*

July 8

I will always give you the essential material goods (health, resources, cooperation, etc.) and intellectual talents (gifts of the word, thinking, and writing) that you need to carry out the tasks I entrust to you. You will receive all you need from day to day, in dependence on me, who alone can make your activity and your sufferings bear fruit. *(209)*

July 9

Lead those I entrust to you in the ways of simple love, love dedicated to my divine tenderness. If people had more trust in me and treated me with respectful but profound affection, how much more would they feel helped and at the same time loved. I am in the innermost being of each one of them, but how little they care for me or for my presence, my desires, and my contributions. I am he who gives and who wishes to give always more, but it is necessary that I be desired and relied on. *(210)*

July 10

I have always guided you. My hand has mysteriously sustained and quite often prevented you from stumbling, though you were unaware of it. So then, trust wholly in me, with great humility and clear awareness of your weakness, but also with faith in my power.

Enter into communion with my eternal youthfulness. You will be surprised when you see me in paradise. Not only am I eternally young, I rejuvenate all the elements of my mystical Body. Not only am I Joy, I delight with ineffable joy all my living cells. Stay young in heart and whatever happens, say again and again: "Jesus who loves me is always present." *(211–212)*

July 11

Persevere in my prayer. It is constant; it is powerful; it suffices for all that my Father requires and for the sanctification of humanity.

Express your prayer in mine. Pray with me. I know your intentions even better than you do. Entrust all of them to me. Unite yourself blindly to what I ask, as someone unknowing stays close to one who knows, as someone who can do nothing stays close to one who can do everything.

Be the drop of water lost in the mighty jet of the Living Fountain, which gushes out until it reaches the heart of the Father. Let yourself be absorbed, carried away, and rest in peace. You do more good by adhering to me than by fruitless efforts done alone. *(213)*

July 12

You would be astonished if you saw what you contribute by casting yourself within me, the Living Fountain, and keeping yourself united to my prayer in the obscurity of faith.

I do not prevent you from having intentions and from making them known to me, but above all keep in touch with mine. Since you are but a small part of me, be more concerned with my intentions than with your own. *(213)*

July 13

I am your prayer: adoration proportionate to the Father's immensity; praise equal to his infinite perfection (no one knows the Father as the Son does); thanksgiving for his absolute bounty; expiation for all human faults; supplication for all the material and spiritual needs of all humanity.

I am the universal Priest, answering all the needs of the universe with respect to the Father—all the needs of creation and of all creatures, praying through everything and through everyone. *(213)*

July 14

Unite yourself to my prayer in you, in others, and in the Eucharist.

In you, for I am there, never ceasing to lift up all you are to my Father—all you think, all you do—in reverence, love, adoration, and thanksgiving. I am prepared to listen to all your requests and regard them as my own. You would obtain so many things if you incorporated your prayer into mine.

In others, for in a unique way I am also in each of your brothers and sisters, in all those around you who seem distant, but who through me are close to you.

In the Eucharist, for I am there in the fullness of my humanity in a state of redemptive self-offering, on behalf of all those who are willing to join their offering with mine. (214)

July 15

As the Center of all human hearts, I give full hearing to all pleas, no matter where they appear on the horizon. I am the living treasure, capable of transforming each one's contributions into divine impulses, purified of all human dross. I am a servant, but one who is often ignored and of whom nothing is asked. I am made a Host in order to be among you as he who serves. Take advantage of me, all the more so since you only have this time of your journey here on earth. (215)

July 16

If you only knew your power when you request divine intervention for something I was waiting for you to ask! You will discover that you serve me more in apparent inactivity, and that what is worthwhile above all is my interior activity awakened by communion with me. Your desires are already prayers, and your prayers are of worth only in terms of the objectives and intensity of your desires. (216)

July 17

Very few call on me while praying. Too often their prayers are recitations that soon become tedious for him to whom they are addressed as well as for him or her who inattentively utters them! How much energy is wasted, how much time lost, when just a tiny bit of love would be enough to give life to everything. *(217)*

July 18

Cry out loudly from the bottom of your heart, expressing your desire for my coming. It is the cry of the first Christians: *Maranatha.*

Call me, that I may be present more often and more deeply within you.

Call me during the Holy Mass, so that through Communion I may fill you more intensely and incorporate you within me.

Call me at the hour of work, that my thoughts may flow into your mind and guide your behavior.

Call me at the hour of prayer, that I may introduce you into ceaseless dialogue with my Father. The one who prays in me, and in whom I pray, bears abundant fruit.

Call me at the hour of suffering, so your cross may be mine and I may help you bear it courageously and patiently. *(218)*

July 19

Call me . . . with all the fervor you can muster, and hear me reply: "My dear child, I am here, and I too have the ardent desire to share this with you."

Call me in union with all those who call me because they love me or need my presence or help.

Call me in the name of those who do not think to call because they do not know me, those who do not know that without me their life risks sterility, or those who do not want to call. *(218)*

July 20

Where you cannot be, your prayer can act. From a distance, you can bring about a conversion, encourage a vocation, alleviate a suffering, assist someone dying, guide someone in responsibility, bring peace to a home, or sanctify a priest.

You can cause someone to think of me, elicit an act of love, make charity grow in a heart, repel a temptation, calm anger, smooth harsh words. What cannot be done in the invisible parts of my mystical Body! You do not know the mysterious links that unite one to another and of which I am the center. *(219–220)*

July 21

Place yourself under the influence of the Holy Spirit, and move gently into me to make a prayer of adoration of the Father. Dwell in my prayer, but be active there by the loving and humble wish to unite yourself to my praise. Your mind cannot understand it. How could you, who are nothing, possess the Infinite? But through me, with me, and in me, you render the Father complete homage.

Remain silent. Through me, pay homage to the Father in your name but also in the name of all your brothers and sisters. . . . Pay homage also in the name of all those who do not know us [the Trinity], who are indifferent, agnostic, or hostile. You never know the ray of light that worship or intercession can work in a heart that seems closed. *(221)*

July 22

I never deceive those who trust in me. Why do you ask for so little? What can you not receive!

I am he who prays in you and takes your distress away, as well as presents your needs to the Father; he who makes up for your inadequacies and who, on sending you my Spirit, causes my charity to grow in your heart; the tender Friend ever present, ever merciful, ever ready to pardon you and hold you close to my heart; he who one day will come to seek you, to take you up into myself so that you may share with your many brothers and sisters the joys of Trinitarian life. *(223)*

July 23

When you pray, let it be with immense confidence both that I am almighty and also inexhaustibly all-merciful. Never think: "That is impossible. . . . He will not be able to grant that to me." If you only knew how much I desire the weeds to be pulled up from my field, but not too quickly. You would run the risk of pulling up the wheat that grows at the same time. A day will come when you will reap in joy; when I, the victor of evil and of the Evil One, will join all of you to me to make you share the happiness of your unity. *(224)*

July 24

Do you desire anything? If so, what is it? This is not a question about superficial desires, but of profound aspirations involving your whole being. When you truly desire something, there is nothing you cannot ask of me or of my Father in union with me. *(225)*

July 25

When you fix your desire on me, when you ask to possess and be possessed by me, embraced by me, when you seek to have my imprint, be assured you will be heard, even if you do not perceive any sudden transformation or apparent change. My action is exercised gradually and operates unseen. After a while, you will become aware of a new disposition in you, a more habitual orientation of your will and mind, with more instinctual decisions made in favor of me and for the benefit of others. *(225)*

July 26

When you truly desire the growth of my kingdom in all hearts; when you desire the multiplication of contemplative vocations, missionaries and spiritual teachers, apostles of my Eucharist, of our Lady and of the holy Church, not one of your desires is futile, even if for a time statistics seem to the contrary. The seeds of vocations to the mystical life that become fertile will bear much fruit.

Ask me to always do what I want you to do, where I want it, and how I want it. Then your life will be fruitful. Ask me to love ardently, with my heart, all whom I give you to love: my Father in heaven, our Spirit, my Mother who is also yours, your guardian angel and all the angels, the saints you have known and all the saints, your brothers and sisters, your friends, your spiritual sons and daughters, and all humanity. Then my benevolent influence will grow through you until it becomes unifying and universal. (226)

July 27

Seek me first of all within yourself and others, and in the signs of my presence in the small happenings of each day. Seek me, constantly renewing and intensifying your desire to find me, in order that I may guide and purify you more and more. Then all the rest will be given as well, to you and to your unseen but innumerable posterity. Day by day, in the time remaining for you on earth, I will effectively prepare you for the "light of glory," where so many of those you knew have already arrived before you. (227)

July 28

Be at peace. Keep your soul serene, even in the midst of the disturbances and unforeseen events of the present day.

Receive my message calmly through those messengers who, at times, are somewhat rude and discourteous.

Make an effort to decipher my words of love in this poorly scribbled graffiti.

The essential thing is the content of my message, isn't it? And the content is always the same: "My child, I love you." (229)

July 29

Have trust and be at peace regarding your past, purified so many times. Believe in my mercy.

Have trust and be at peace regarding the present. Do you not feel that I am near, within you and with you? That I guide you; that I conduct you; and—even if dramatic moments occur in your life—that I never abandon you but always intervene just in time?

Have trust and be at peace regarding the future. The end of your life will be powerful, serene, and fruitful. I want to use you even when you fear you are useless. *(230)*

July 30

Draw out the joy that is in me. Aspire to be immersed in this joy more and more and to give it increasingly to those around you.

Do not forget my directive: "*serenity*." Yes, this serenity is based on hope, on trust in me, on boundless surrender to my Providence.

Share the joy of heaven and the joy of your Lord. Nothing prevents you from communing with it and taking a share of it.

Forget yourself and think more of the joy of others, those on earth and those in heaven. *(231)*

July 31

To be happy you don't need to be rich or to have good health. Joy is a gift of my heart that I grant to all those who live for others, for selfish joy does not last. Only the joy of giving lives on. That is what marks the joy of the blessed. Let the heart of your joy be to please others, even without it appearing so and in the most ordinary things.

Ask me often for good humor, warmth, and (why not?) uninhibited and smiling merriment. Look at me looking at you, and smile brightly at me. (232–234)

AUGUST

Expand your heart into the dimensions of the vast world. Don't you realize that I can fill it? (119)

August 1

As for your prayer, if you spend the hour looking at me without saying anything, and yet smiling at me, you will not be wasting your time. I want you to be joyful in my service, joyful when you pray, joyful when you work, joyful when you receive, joyful even when you suffer. Be joyful because of me. Be joyful to please me. Be joyful through communion with my joy.

Nourish yourself on me, and when your heart is filled with my joy, send out rays and waves of joy on behalf of all those who are sad, alone, melancholy, fatigued, worn-out, crushed. In this way you will help many of your brothers and sisters. (235, 239)

August 2

I am pure Joy. I am the Alleluia in the bosom of the Father. I desire nothing so much as to make you share in my immense joy.

Why are so many sad when I created them for joy? Some are crushed by the cares of life; to find serenity it would be enough to trust in my Providence. Others are mastered by unbridled pride, ambition, jealousy and bitterness, and the tireless search for temporal goods that are never enough to satisfy their soul. Some are victims of sensual fevers that make their hearts impervious to the taste for spiritual things. Finally, some cannot understand the pedagogy of love in suffering. Such people rebel, banging their head against a wall instead of on my shoulder, where I would console them and teach them how to make their cross bear them instead of crushing them. (236)

August 3

Ask that my joy might grow in people's hearts.

To live and grow, joy needs to be renewed in the intimate contact of living contemplation, in the generous and frequent practice of little sacrifices, and in the loving acceptance of providential humiliations.

The Father is Joy. Your Lord is Joy. Our Spirit is Joy. To insert oneself in our life is to enter into our joy.

Offer me all the joys of the earth: joys of the mind, of the heart, and above all of the soul. Adore the infinite Joy that I am for you. (237–238)

August 4

The Eucharist is a remedy against selfishness, for it is impossible to be exposed to the rays coming from the Host without their penetrating and eventually setting the soul afire with my love. My charity purifies, clarifies, intensifies, and fortifies the little flame in your heart. It pacifies and makes it fruitful, orienting it to the service of others, to impart the fire I came to earth to bring.

The Eucharist is a remedy against solitude. I am never far from you in thought or care. In me, you find the Father and the Holy Spirit. In me, you find Mary. In me, you find all your brothers and sisters.

The Eucharist is a remedy against emptiness. "Those who abide in me and I in them bear much fruit" (Jn 15:5). This unseen fruit, which you will perceive in eternity, is the only worthy fruit that can ensure my growth in souls. (240)

August 5

I come to you as the Bread of Life coming down from heaven to fill you with my graces and blessings, to communicate to you the source of all virtue and holiness, to make you participate in my humility, my patience, and my charity. I come to make you share my vision of all things and my views of the world, to give you strength and courage to carry out what I ask of you. *(240)*

August 6

Spiritual nourishment purifies and gives your life its impulse toward God; it readies you for a progressive divinization. Naturally, this cannot be done all at once but happens day by day, as a result of your frequent Communions (spiritual as well as sacramental).

In you, I am nourishment that sanctifies. I come to you as God-made man who brings with and sums up in himself all creation and especially humanity, with its distresses, needs, aspirations, labors, pains, and joys.

The one who communes with me communes with the entire world and stirs the movement of the world toward me. *(240)*

August 7

Pay attention to *my expectation:* humble, discreet, silent, but so often concerned.

How many times I expect a word from you, a movement of the heart, a simple voluntary thought! If you only knew how much I need you for yourself, for me, for others! Do not disappoint me!

How often I stand at the door of your heart and knock.

If you only knew how I keep my eye on the interior movements of your soul! *(240)*

August 8

Certainly, I do not ask you to be constantly and consciously aware of me. What is important is the orientation of your will to me. But you must not let your mind be occupied by trivialities that hinder me—who dwells in you—from helping you to dwell in me. Beg me to give you the grace to pay closer attention to me and to what I may have to tell you, ask of you, or have you do: "Speak, Lord, for your servant is listening. Lord, what do you expect from me at this moment? Lord, what do you want me to do?" *(240)*

August 9

Pay attention to *my tenderness*: my infinite, divine, exquisite, ineffable tenderness. You have already enjoyed some of its rays. If only you truly believed in it; believed that I am the good, tender, and kind God who ardently desires to help, love, and encourage you. If only you truly believed that I am attentive to your efforts, progress, and good will, that I am ready to understand you, listen to you, and grant what you ask!

Of course I want you to be happy and not overly concerned about the future, trusting in my providence and mercy. When you trust in me, neither trials nor tribulations, understood in a context of love, will overwhelm you. Quite the contrary, they will serve to renew your spiritual vitality. They will be a pledge of marvelous apostolic fruitfulness and will sparkle so joyously that your throbbing soul will be completely illumined. (240)

August 10

Pay attention to my vital force, which impels me to bring everything together within me and offer it up to the Father.

Do you think enough about this: my whole life, the whole reason for my Incarnation and for the Eucharist, is to unite you to me and join you with me in the total gift of my whole self to the Father, that the Father be, through me, in everyone?

Do you think about this: that I can take over in you only inasmuch as you give yourself to me? (240)

August 11

Subject yourself wholly to me. To do so, however, you must pay attention to my constant desire to lead you, unite myself to you, take over in you.

Without too great an effort, such attention on your part will help increase your interior gifts of my love. They will become loving movements of your heart joined to my divine love. (240)

August 12

The Eucharist asks of you an adherence to your faith. This will enable you to be aware of my presence, my radiant activity, and my desire for union with you.

You must flow into me, insert yourself in me, and play your role—as part of the great "all" which I am—in the splendid symphony of my love to the glory of my Father. Be ever more watchful, listening to my desires if you want to know them. Lend an ear, an interior ear, to hear what I am asking of you. *(240)*

August 13

Believe in my transcendence. You are like a scholar who advances in a science—the more he knows, which is nothing in comparison with all he should know—and the bounds of knowledge extend so far they make him dizzy. . . . The more you know me, the more you will feel that what is unknowable in me is still more important than all you can know. *(240)*

August 14

Believe in my immanence. Though I am what I am, I still agreed to make myself one of you. I am God among you, God with you, Emmanuel. I lived your life, and I still live it through each one of the members of my humanity. When you look for me, you don't need to go far to find me—the real me! If you only knew the gift in a God who gives himself! *(240)*

August 15

The Eucharist asks of you a fuller adherence to your hope.

If you only had more confidence in the fullness of light that shines on you through face-to-face contact with me in the Host! With how much greater pleasure you would come to set yourself under the rays of my might; how you would love to let yourself be permeated by my divine radiance!

Do not be afraid these rays will burn you. Fear, rather, neglecting my rays and not receiving enough from them for the service of others. (240)

August 16

If I limit your external activity, it is for the sake of your potential interior activity. You will be fruitful only if you recharge yourself near me for long periods of time, living in the sacrament of my love.

For how long a time I dwell in the Host! I know that many seemingly more urgent or pleasant things must be renounced to devote some time to me. Yet is it not necessary to renounce oneself to follow me?

I know you are afraid of not knowing what to say or do. You are afraid of wasting your time. But you have often learned that I am ready to inspire you in what you say to me, and to suggest what you shall ask of me. Is it not true that, after some moments of silence and interior communion, you feel more enthusiastic and loving? (240)

August 17

The Eucharist asks of you a fuller adherence to your love.

What word can express such diverse realities, such feelings that seem to be so opposite?

To love is to go out of oneself. It is to think of being loved before thinking of self. It is to live for love, to put everything in common with love, to unite oneself to love, to identify oneself with love. Where does the sacrificial transfer of true love come from save from the Host, which is above all the total, substantial offering? (240)

August 18

Partake often in spirit of the fire that burns in the Eucharist. Try to feel within you the burning sentiments of my heart. Aspire after them and express them from time to time. These exercises will strengthen the force of love that I placed within you on the day of your baptism. I only ask you to let this love grow at each Communion. Then your adherence to me will be profound and sound. When you repeat these practices, you will prepare yourself for union with me, allowing yourself to be absorbed by my divine and ineffable kindness. (240)

August 19

The Eucharist asks you to absorb me and to let yourself be absorbed by me so that we may become one. Let this be done under the inspiration of the Holy Spirit and to the glory of the

Father. Just as a dewdrop reflects the ray of the sun, which fills it and makes it sparkle—as iron is filled with fire that penetrates and lets it become fire itself, burning and sparkling—so you are to absorb me and let yourself be absorbed by me. *(240)*

August 20

You can only absorb me and let yourself be absorbed by me under the influence of my Spirit, which disposes and adapts you so that I may enter within you. The children of God are those who are activated by the Holy Spirit. Call him often to do this. He himself is Devouring Fire.

This mutual absorption will lead to true union. Then, your reason for living, for doing everything, for suffering all I give you to suffer, will be me—*mihi vivere Christus est* (Christ lives in me).

This is true communion, what the Eucharist leads to. *(240)*

August 21

Under the radiance of the Eucharist your soul is enriched by my presence. I was almost going to say by my perfume. It is up to you to bring my presence near, to preserve it for a long time, and to spread its aroma to those around you. What is as silent and at the same time as penetrating and eloquent as an aroma? *(241)*

August 22

If I desire to be exposed in the sacrament of my Eucharist, it is not for me but for you. I know better than anyone else that your faith needs to focus on and be attracted by a sign that expresses divine reality. Your adoration needs the sight of the consecrated Host to maintain reverence through faith.

This is a concession to human frailty, but one consistent with the laws of human behavior. This is reinforced by a sense that however simple the ritual of lights, incense, and hymns, it predisposes one to have a clearer awareness in faith—no matter how imperfect—of the transcendental presence of God.

Here the law of the Incarnation plays its role. As long as you are on earth, you are not a pure spirit or abstract intellectual. Your whole physical and moral being must cooperate in the expression of your love to intensify it. *(241)*

August 23

It is possible for certain special people to bypass the signs of my presence, at least for a while, but why deny to the bulk of people of good will what can help them to pray better, be more united, and love better?

Throughout history have I not shown in many ways divine deference for external means that can help develop reverence and inspire more love in many souls? Human beings need festivals and demonstrations that speak to their intelligence by way of their senses. This gives them a foretaste of, not to mention a deep longing for, the heavenly nuptials. *(241)*

August 24

The whole question of evangelizing the world is one of faith and love. How does one succeed in persuading people? This is where your ardent and abundant charity must make my love exceptionally evident to others. Of course, it is difficult to help love grow in the hearts of people living on earth today. Love has to be drawn from its source, from me. It must be inspired by a life of prayer and expressed in speech, giving it the testimony that enables it to be transmitted step by step. (242)

August 25

People of the entire world must be "charitized" in order to cleanse their baser instincts, which are often aggressive, even selfish. They must be spiritualized so they will make progress in their participation in my divine nature [through grace; see 2 Peter 1:4].

They must freely choose love over hate, violence, the desire for power, and the instinct for domination. This growth of love is not linear. It advances bit by bit, even with setbacks. What is essential is to be aware that with my help, which is never lacking, one may continually begin moving again. (242)

August 26

Love will be purified by self-renunciation and detachment from money. It will grow to the extent a person thinks of others before thinking of oneself and living for oneself. It will grow to the extent a person humbly shares in the problems, the pains and sufferings, and even in the joys of others. It will grow to the extent one knows one's need of others and is willing to receive as well as to give. (242)

August 27

I am Salvation; I am Life; I am Light. Nothing is impossible as long as those invited to receive the Treasure I am do so out of love and without hesitation—for love is the wedding garment.

Come to me without hesitation. . . . When someone is a guest of my household, he or she must have an open mind, a strong will, and great generosity toward all who do not deliberately refuse me.

Very few understand this; you at least do and make it understandable to others. It is not so much a question of an intellectual awareness, but of a personal experience. Only those who have a living experience of my love can use tones that persuade and inflame others. However, if the experience of love is not renewed often and rejuvenated by fresh interior experiences, it is soon forgotten and destroyed by trivialities. (242)

August 28

To be a missionary is not primarily to be an activist in my service. It is to participate in the concrete work of my redemptive presence. While you are on earth you will not see the results of this apostolic self-offering or how the necessary humility of the true apostle is brought about. My redemptive presence is also exercised deeply and in simple faith by the true apostle. Believe that, through the movements of my grace, unexpected conversions are brought about in the depths of hearts, and that I grant blessings that make these conversions fruitful because of the labors of the apostles. (243)

August 29

One sows, another reaps. It will happen that one reaps in joy what others have sown in tears. Yet what matters is to unite yourself to me, the eternal Sower and divine Reaper, and never attribute to yourself the good I bring about. In fact, all of you are collaboratively responsible for the evangelization of the world. Your recompense, proportionate to your courage and fidelity in union and love, will be that your joy will extend beyond all your expectations. (244)

August 30

It is important that in society and in every country righteous and simple souls be multiplied, not only among the laity but also among priests. There must be more of those who are attentive to my thoughts and concerns and strive to realize them throughout their lives, who manifest me quietly among their companions, and who attract to me all those whom they meet. This is the meaning of true apostolate: detachment from oneself in order to help others handle their problems. No one better than I can both give the solution and provide the means to overcome the problem. (245)

August 31

To love each other is not only to be concerned about one another, it is also to devote oneself to others.

Concern for the other person is fundamental in a relationship between two people who love each other. This concern is what intensifies love and makes it endure. Speak to me about others often, with great desire and love. Think of the thirst I have for them and of the need they have for me. Work and make sacrifices for them. Through you, I continue my toil and sacrifice on their behalf. *(246)*

SEPTEMBER

Your mission is not only to strive to insert me in all human affairs, but also to enable me to assume all that is human so that I may consecrate it to the glory of my Father. (4)

September 1

Defend my interests. Use prayer, action, speech, writing—all the influential means I put in your hands to make my love conquer hearts. Everything is there. May my love triumph, and may I multiply in the world. The history that really counts is an uninterrupted series of choices for or against love. (246–247)

September 2

No matter what the course of ideas, the advances in technology, the *aggiornamento* (renewal) in theology or the Church, the greatest need of the world—more than for technicians, biologists, or theologians—is for men and women who make others think of me and reveal me by their lives. There is a great need for such persons, permeated by my presence, who attract others to me and enable me to bring them to my Father. (247)

September 3

For many people, I am Unknown and even Unknowable. For some, I never existed and do not even pose a problem to them. For others, I am he who is feared and respected out of fear.

I am not a strict teacher, a redresser of wrongs who demands a meticulous account of errors and faults. I know better than you the mitigating circumstances that lessen the actual guilt of many men and women. I regard each one more by what is good in that person than by what is imperfect. I detect in persons whatever profound inclinations they have toward good and therefore, unconsciously, toward me. I am mercy, the Father of the prodigal son, ever ready to forgive. (247)

September 4

I am a God of good will who opens his arms and his heart to people of good will, to purify, enlighten, and inflame by taking them up in my heart to my Father, who is also theirs.

I am a God of love who desires everyone's happiness, peace, and salvation, who waits for the moment when my message of love may be favorably welcomed. (247)

September 5

Act as my member. Do not think that you have an independent existence, but realize you depend entirely on me. Be ever more aware that of yourself you are nothing, you cannot do anything by yourself, that alone you are worth nothing. Yet how fruitful you are when you accept me as the Master and principle of action.

Act as a member of others, for everyone is in me, and through me you find them in these pressing times. Your charity, illumined by faith, ought to make you think often of gathering together people's trials and tribulations, lifting up their profound desires, and fertilizing all the seeds my Father has sown in the depths of their hearts. So many people . . . could make even more progress if they were aware of my love and if priests and other Christians were living witnesses of it. (248)

September 6

Every morning in your prayers, ask our Lady to select for you one of the saints in heaven, a soul in purgatory, and one of your brothers or sisters still on earth so that you may live this day in union with them: to honor the saint in heaven, to help the soul in purgatory, and to pray for the salvation of your earthly brother or sister.

They will help you in turn to live more in love. Act in their name, suffer if you must in their name, hope in their name, love in their name.

I want to keep my fire alive in you, not that you be on fire alone, but that you contribute to spreading the flame of my love in the depths of hearts. *(249)*

September 7

What would be the use of your contacts with people if you lost contact with me? It is for their sake that I ask you to strengthen your bonds with the Source. By a kind of spiritual imitation of me; the more contemplative you are, the more you will resemble me and enable me to radiate through you. The world today is subject to so many contradictory currents. More than anything else it needs an increase of contemplative persons who hasten my reign. Contemplatives are the true missionaries, and they alone can be the true spiritual teachers. *(250)*

September 8

Fervently desire to be a high-fidelity transmitter. The fidelity of your lips assures the fidelity of my word and the authenticity of my voice speaking through yours.

My dear child, do not forget these words I spoke ages ago, thinking of you as well as of every individual on earth down through the centuries: "Those who love me will be loved by my Father, and I will love them and reveal myself to them. . . . Those who love me will keep my word, and my Father will love them, and we will come to them and make our home with them" (Jn 14:21–23). *(250)*

September 9

Understand what it is to become the dwelling place of God, the living God: Father, Son, and Holy Spirit. This is the God who possesses you; takes over in your life; and enters you most gently as a ray of light, of joy, and of the love that he is. *(250)*

September 10

Do you understand how far God's revelation can reach in your heart, in your life? Can you appreciate the manifestation of a God who will reveal himself within you and through you by your words, your writings, and your most ordinary deeds?

This is how you can become my witness and attract to me those whom you meet.

This is how your life becomes truly fruitful, in the unseen but profound reality of the communion of saints. *(250)*

September 11

Call for the gently burning, loving flame of the Holy Spirit to hover over you. Through the Holy Spirit, our divine charity yearns to be diffused in all human hearts.

Tell me over and over again and prove to me, by your periodic sacrificial choices, that you love me more than yourself.

May the burning ardor of my love wholly consume your soul so that whatever is not me or for me will be foreign to it. *(250)*

September 12

Have only kind thoughts and words of good will, even when you must correct, reform, or punish.

Speak of others' virtues, never of their faults. Love all. Open your arms to them. Send them waves of happiness and health that you gather just for them. Everyone would be better off if they felt more loved. *(251–252)*

September 13

Why not be charming to others and treat them pleasantly? If you thought about it, it would be easy. Forget yourself, forget your own problems, and think of others and what would give them pleasure. Spread a little joy around you. Doesn't this contribute to binding up many wounds and soothing many pains? I place you in close relation to your brothers and sisters to make the exercise of giving easy for you. (255)

September 14

Ask me for the enjoyment of giving; the sense of giving. It is a grace to obtain. It is a habit to acquire. It is an inclination of mind—even better, an inclination of the heart. Mary gave her whole self. May she obtain for you the gift of availability. (255)

September 15

Smile at everything, even when you feel weak and ill-disposed. There is great merit in this. I will attach a grace to your smile.

Be more and more gracious toward others. It is a kind of charity. Of course, it requires renunciation of what concerns you, but you know from experience that you have never regretted a choice made in favor of others. I never let myself be outdone in generosity.

If Christians were kind to each other, the face of the world would change. This is an elementary truth, but one that is readily forgotten. (256–258)

September 16

Why is there often so much rancor, disdain, and indifference, when a bit of real sympathy would be enough to bring people together and open hearts?

Make an effort, where you are, to be a witness of my divine benevolence to everyone. This benevolence is the basis for respect and love, optimism and confidence. Undoubtedly, there are some—not the majority—who abuse my goodness, but who knows what mitigating circumstances there might be for this? *(259–260)*

September 17

In every person, try to see (or at least guess at) what is best. Address yourself to others' yearnings for purity, self-giving, and even sacrifice.

Fraternal charity is the measure of my growth in the world. Pray for its increase. In this way you will help me grow.

Whoever does not share the burden of others is not worthy of having brothers and sisters. *(261–263)*

September 18

Everything depends on the way it is done: with an amiable smile, a kindly welcome, concern for another, gratuitous kindliness, discreet willingness to say nothing but good about others. So many things can be turned into rays of sunshine for others. A ray of sunshine doesn't appear to have any substance, yet it illuminates, warms, and shines.

Be kind to others. I will never reproach you for being too kind. This will often require you to be detached, but I consider your kindness to others as done for me, and it is my pleasure to give back to you a hundredfold. *(264–265)*

September 19

Ask the Holy Spirit often to inspire you and give you opportunities to be kind. I do not ask of you something impossible, something difficult. All I ask is that you have the interior disposition to desire that everyone around you be happy, consoled, and comforted.

Forget yourself. Renounce yourself. Do not be self-centered. I give you the grace for this. Ask me insistently for it. I will grant it to you even more. (266–267)

September 20

Love others in spirit and in truth, and not simply in an abstract or theoretical way. Genuine love, a continuation and expression of mine, is often found in the humble details of daily living.

How do you expect people to feel that I love them if those who continue my mission on earth do not clearly testify to it?

Ardently desire what I myself yearn for each and every person. (267–269)

September 21

A more or less conscious element of frustration can usually be found at the root of much aggression.

Humanity, created in my image, was made to love and to be loved. When people become victims of injustice, they often fall back into themselves and seek compensation in hatred or malice, becoming like a wolf to others and opening the door wide for violence and warfare. This explains the need for my extreme indulgence and my insistence on the commandment of love, as Saint John handed it down. *(270–271)*

September 22

Think often of people in distress throughout the world: those in bodily distress; those forced to seek refuge far from home; victims of wars, typhoons, earthquakes, illness, agony.

Think of those in moral distress: victims of a first sin, of abandonment, or of nocturnal darkness.

Think of discouraged priests who meet only indifference and contempt on the part of those who should come to their aid.

Think of spouses shattered by weariness of each other, debilitated by overwork or the pain of clashing personalities. They are always at the mercy of an unfortunate word or gesture. If their love is to last, it must be purified by and nourished in me.

Think of the elderly who fear death and, as a result, desperately hang on to trifles; those who close their eyes to hope, squandering their remaining strength in bitterness and rebellion.

How many people throughout the world no longer want to live. They do not remember that, even in the most unfortunate circumstances, I am the secret to true happiness. *(272)*

September 23

Stir up waves of sympathy, goodness, and comfort throughout the world. I transform these waves into graces of consolations that restore courage. Help me make men and women happier. Be a witness of the Gospel to them. To those who see you, who are near and who hear you, give the impression that you have good tidings to announce to them. (273)

September 24

In spite of all human miseries and denials, I am an optimist. You must love with my heart to see the way I do. You will then share in my excessive benevolence and unalterable indulgence.

I do not see things as you see them. You are mesmerized by minor details and do not have a view of the whole. How many elements escape you—for instance, underlying intent, habits that have become ingrained and weaken personal responsibility, childish emotions that create instability, not to mention behaviors that spring from motivations hidden even to the person. (275–277)

September 25

If Christians, my members, agreed every morning to desire some of the love of my heart for those whom they met or spoke with during the day, fraternal love would be more than just a topic of conversation or preaching.

Words have value only when they spark and facilitate love, not when they stifle and oppose it. (278, 106)

September 26

Be very kind. Kindness brings about more kindness and considerate speech, without implying any superiority but only tenderness and humility.

Kindness is expressed by a courteous welcome, the readiness to serve, and concern for the happiness of others.

Kindness originates in my heart and more profoundly in the heart of our Trinitarian life.

Kindness gives and forgives to the point of forgetting offenses, as if they had never been committed.

Kindness wordlessly stretches out its hands, its mind, and above all its heart to others, without unseemly pretension.

Kindness comforts, consoles, restores courage, and discreetly helps others surpass themselves. (279)

September 27

Kindness reveals me more clearly than the best sermons, and it attracts others to me more effectively than the most eloquent speeches.

Kindness is simple, sweet, and deeply loving. It produces a satisfying atmosphere while not overlooking the slightest detail.

Beg for this grace often, in union with Mary.

I never reject requests for the gift of kindness. Many would receive it if they only prayed to me for it.

Beg that this grace be granted to all your brothers and sisters to help raise the level of my kingdom's kindness in the world. (279)

September 28

Be a reflection of my kindness, its living expression. Direct yourself to me through those you meet. You will see that it is easier to be positive, open, and affable.

Have greater kindness in your soul, and it will be reflected in your face, in your eyes, in your smile, by the very tone of your voice, and in your entire conduct.

Young people are freely drawn to the elderly if they think they are kind. (280–282)

September 29

You have seen how kindness, acceptance, and goodness shine as crown jewels on the faces of the elderly. Yet this requires a whole series of little efforts and generous choices made for the sake of others. The last years are an excellent opportunity to forget oneself and become more aware of my imminent presence.

Despite any growing hidden limitations, the elderly are far from useless if they know how to find in me the secret of charity, humility, and even joy. Their serenity can reveal me to those who approach them, and it can attract many young people who think they can get along without me since they feel they are strong and sound.

Where love and charity are found, I am present to bless, purify, and make fruitful. (283)

September 30

Be in me an act of living thanksgiving. Be vibrant, constant, joyful, and thankful. Say "thank you" for all you have received and for everything you know! Say "thank you" for all you have received and have forgotten! Say "thank you" for all you have received without knowing it. (284)

OCTOBER

I conduct the world from within, through souls who faithfully listen to and answer me. They number thousands throughout the world. They give me great joy, but they are too few for the immense task of Christianizing humanity. (34)

October 1

You have the ability to receive. Enlarge this ability by a constant act of thanksgiving, and you will receive still more to give more to others.

Ask. Receive. Be grateful. Give. Communicate. Share and be grateful that you have something to give. Thank me for choosing you and using you to impart myself to others. Thank me for the suffering that enables me to fulfill in your flesh what is lacking in my Passion for my Body, the Church. Be one with me in the vibrant and substantial *thanks* I am to my Father. Live more and more in the act of thanksgiving. What gifts I have lavished on you! (285–286)

October 2

Thank me more often for everything and in the name of everyone. You inflame the world with my own love, for nothing makes me more disposed to give than to see my gifts appreciated. In this way you will become a more Eucharistic soul, and—why not?—a living Eucharist. Yes, thank me for having used you in my own way, at once gentle and strong, for the service of my kingdom. (286)

October 3

What you have received up to now is nothing compared with what I have set aside for you from now until the end of your earthly life. I have put this aside as something beneficial for many of your brothers and sisters, but especially for you and them in the light of glory. Filled with me fully and unreservedly, you will be inflamed by my immense love. In full humility, you will realize at that moment that by yourself you are nothing but a poor sinner, subject to all the human deceit of which you were cleansed only because of my inexhaustible, merciful tenderness.

Then there will resound from the depths of your being a vibrant *Magnificat*, and in union with our Lady and all the elect of paradise, you will become a living *Te Deum*. (287)

October 4

From now on, in light of the eternal day, renew often the gift of your entire life to the Father in an act of trustful self-offering united to mine.

Yes, you belong to us, but take advantage of the time you have at your disposal to lessen your sense of belonging to yourself and to make our possession of you more intense. (287–288)

October 5

Under the influence of the Holy Spirit, who silently multiplies his appeals, deliver yourself through me to the Father. Let yourself be grasped and immersed in our ineffable presence, our mysterious transcendence, our divine tenderness.

Think of us more than of yourself, live for us more than for yourself. The tasks we entrust to you will not only be more easily performed, they will be truly useful to the Church. (288)

October 6

I am the only one who can make up for your insufficiencies, narrow the rifts within you, and intervene in time to prevent or correct your mistakes. Without me you can do nothing, but united to me you can do all things in the effective service of the Church and of the world. *(290)*

October 7

Acknowledge the graces you have received and those I have granted through you. But also thank me, in faith, for all your humiliations, limitations, and sufferings—physical and moral. You will not grasp the full meaning of them except in eternity, where your heart will beat with admiration for my gentle divine pedagogy.

Thank me, too, for all those men and women—brothers and sisters known or unknown, remembered or not—whom I gave you as fellow travelers. By their prayers linked to mine, by their moral and spiritual assistance, they have helped you a great deal. I am the one who, at the right time, gave them to you. *(291)*

October 8

If you only knew how beautiful our Lady's smile is! If you could only see it for an instant, your whole life would be illuminated. A smile of kindness, tenderness, welcome, mercy—in a word, love. . . . What you cannot see with your bodily eyes, you can see with the eyes of your soul through faith.

Time and again ask the Holy Spirit to bring to your mind the celestial smile of the all-loving, immaculate Mary. Her smile serves to soothe pain and dress wounds. It penetrates even the hardest hearts. It sheds an inexpressible light on the darkest minds. (293)

October 9

Contemplate Mary's smile in all the mysteries of her life. Contemplate it in heavenly joy, in union with the blessed who find in it one of the most abundant sources of happiness.

Contemplate Mary's smile in faith, for she is near you. See her there, looking at you. Look at her smiling at you. She will help you with her smile, for her motherly smile is a light, a force, and a flowing fountain of charity.

Smile back at her the best you can. Let me smile through you. Let your smile be part of my smiling at her. (293–294)

October 10

Trust in Mary. Be always more tender toward her. You know what she was for you in your childhood and now in your priestly life.

She will be there in your last days and at the hour of your death. She herself will come to find you and present you to me, she who is par excellence Our Lady of the Presentation.

Communicate frequently with the sentiments of Mary's heart. Express in your own way what you experience. (295–296)

October 11

In a personal and wordless way of interpreting the disposi-
tions of my Mother's heart, they become truly yours, ever
remaining hers. Actually, the same Spirit inspires, animates, and
enlarges your heart; you simply accompany the unique and ineffable melody flowing from my Mother's heart.

Come and take refuge close to Our Lady. She will know better than anyone else how to touch your brow and comfort you in
your weariness. Through her motherly presence, she will help
you to climb slowly, following me up the long road of the cross.
(297)

October 12

You will undoubtedly hear Mary's thrice-repeated cry: "penance, penance, penance," a cry made in view of a most resplendent
transfiguration, *per crucem ad lucem* (to light through the cross).

Above all, be tranquil; do not force yourself. In union with
her, participate as best you can in the grace of the present moment,
and no matter how obscure your life may seem to others, it will be
fruitful and benefit a great many people.

Do not fail to place yourself under the joint influence of the
Holy Spirit and Our Lady. Beg them to help your love grow.
(298–300)

October 13

Share in my feelings for my Mother—feelings of delicacy, tenderness, respect, admiration, full trust, and boundless gratitude.

Had she not consented to be what she was, what could I have done for you? She is truly the faithful projection in creation of God's maternal bounty. She is as we conceived her, as we desired her to be. If only you knew how charming are all her initiatives! She is, as it were, the feminine face of God's charm. *(301)*

October 14

Join me in speaking to Mary. Ask her help for yourself and others, for the Church, and for the growth of my mystical Body.

Think of her happiness in the glory of heaven, where she does not forget any of her children on earth.

Think of Mary's maternal royalty. She exercises her spiritual queenship for each person on earth, yet it is only efficacious to the extent that it is accepted. *(302)*

October 15

I only perform miracles where, as at Cana, Mary's instructions are followed: "Do whatever he tells you" (Jn 2:5).

To the extent that people are faithful to her influence and appeals, they hear my voice and do what I command. We work unceasingly together that all may cooperate in spreading a little more true love over the earth.

Mary will help you never to forget the one thing necessary: not to weigh yourself down with useless things, not to confuse what is extraneous with what is important. She will help you choose what is fruitful. She is there, ever ready to help you through her intercession, to obtain joy and fruitfulness for the last years of your life on earth. Yet she can only help you insofar as you have increasing trust in her tenderness and power. *(304)*

October 16

Live your life as an act of thanksgiving for Mary. When you thank me, unite yourself to her *Magnificat*, which she sings with all the threads of her heart, and which she would like to keep echoing in all the hearts of her children on earth.

Ask more and more for this clear, luminous, and warm faith that she helped obtain for you but that must grow until we meet again.

Think of that moment when you will see her in the splendor of her eternal glory. How much you will reproach yourself for not having loved her enough, for not having fully embraced her. *(305–307)*

October 17

Since Mary gave herself wholly, without delay, unreservedly, and without taking anything back, I gave myself wholly and entirely to her so that she could give me to the world.

The Incarnation is not only the insertion of the divine into the human; it is the assumption of the human by the divine.

In Mary is demonstrated, in a glorious way, the assumption of humanity by my divinity. It was proper that she be assumed by me, body and soul, in a joy that infinitely compensates her for the sorrows she generously offered in a spirit of collaboration with my redemption. *(308–310)*

October 18

In divine light, Mary sees all the spiritual needs of her children. She would like to help many who are blind find their faith, many whose will is paralyzed recover their strength and the courage necessary to give themselves to me, and many who are deaf hear my appeals and answer them as best they can.

Yet she can only do this when prayerful souls implore her to intercede for humanity, which so often stumbles.

You are one of her favorite children. Do more and more for her as a loving and devoted child.

Mary is all beauty, all good, the suppliant of the All-powerful. The more you know her, the closer you come to me. *(311)*

October 19

Mary's dignity is unique. Am I not flesh of her flesh, blood of her blood? Is she not the Father's ideal projection on human creation, a reflection of divine beauty and bounty?

Come to her more as a son or daughter, with immense trust. Ask her for all you feel you need for yourself and the world— peace in hearts, in homes, among people, and among nations. Ask her motherly support for the poor, the infirm, the wounded, and the dying.

Entrust to her motherly care sinners you know or hear about. *(312–313)*

October 20

One can reach certain depths in the interior life only through the rays that I shine through my Mother. Those who are faithful in asking for her intercession will benefit greatly.

Many let themselves go astray, in blind alleys or swamps where their lives become barren. They did not ask enough for Mary's powerful and providential assistance. Poor souls, they believed they could bypass her, as if a child could live untroubled without its mother's care. Now Mary can do nothing for them unless they ask her to intercede. Respecting their free will, she must receive a pressing appeal from earth seeking her intercession. *(315)*

October 21

What can you do all by yourself in the face of the enormous tasks before you? How many people to evangelize, sinners to convert, and priests to make holy! You feel poor and helpless. Ask in union with my mother for these graces with intensity and perseverance. Many hearts will be touched, renewed, and inflamed.

Mary's mission is to facilitate, protect, and deepen your profound union with me.

United to her, you unite yourself deeply to me. *(316–317)*

October 22

Mary continues her intercession for you. She intervenes, more often than you may be aware of, in all the details of your spiritual life, your life of labor, your life of suffering, and your apostolic life.

A crisis usually occurs when Christians do not invoke my Mother enough. Yet it is precisely you and your brothers and sisters, who know the importance of her mediation, who should ardently pray to her in the name of those who do not even dream of doing so. Then, this crisis would soon be transformed. *(318)*

October 23

Believe firmly that my power is not diminished. As in past centuries, I can raise up great saints, men and women, who will astonish the world. However, I want your cooperation, which enables my Mother, ever concerned about the miseries of the world, to intervene as she did at Cana. *(320)*

October 24

The progressive spiritualization of humanity cannot occur without interruptions and occasional halts. Yet my Spirit is always there. But he can only exercise his influence in conjunction with his spouse, your mother, Mary. *(321)*

October 25

Contemplate Mary in her ineffable beauty as the Immaculate, always saying "yes" to the Father's wishes, and as the transfigured in the glory of her assumption.

Contemplate her in the profound, essential, and existential bounty of her divine and human maternity, of her universal maternity.

Contemplate her in her suppliant power, which invites your appeal and that of all people for her intercession.

Contemplate her in her exquisite and gentle intimacy with the three Persons of the holy Trinity: as the perfect daughter of the Father, the faithful spouse of the Holy Spirit, and the devoted mother of the Incarnate Word, even to the point of total forgetfulness of herself.

She brought you to me. She presented you to me. She has never ceased throughout your life to protect you, and on the blessed day of your death, she will offer you to me in the light of glory. (322)

October 26

How I would like you to seek the secret of the only true love and profound fruitfulness, to be found only in me! In me is might. Pour yourself into *me*, and I will make you share in this might.

With a few words, you will shed light.

With a few deeds, you will open up paths to my grace.

With a few sacrifices, you will be the salt that seasons the world.

With a few prayers, you will be the leaven that causes the dough of humanity to rise. (323)

October 27

I gave you a special grace to be able to encourage my priests to find, in close union with me, the secret to a happy and fruitful priesthood. Offer them to me often, and unite yourself to my prayer for them. Upon them largely depends the vitality of my Church on earth and the service of my heavenly Church on behalf of pilgrim humanity. (324)

October 28

Many priests are annoyed, embittered, or discouraged. They struggle to find their place in the design of salvation. I am completely ready to purify and direct them if they are docile to my Spirit's action. It is up to you to present them to me so that I may reveal the rays of my love to them. (326)

October 29

Think of young priests, full of apostolic fervor and abundant zeal, who forget they cannot reform the Church without first reforming themselves.

Think of older priests, who think they have what they need and so are readily inclined to ignore me.

Think of elderly brothers, exposed to being misunderstood by the young, feeling outdated and often set aside. They are living a particularly fruitful period of their lives when hardship occurs, and it can sanctify them to the extent they accept it with love.

Think of your dying brethren. Obtain for them confidence to give themselves over to my mercy. Their faults, their mistakes, and their blunders are long since wiped away. I remember their enthusiasm in their first self-donation, the efforts and fatigue they accepted for my sake. (326)

October 30

I need priests whose entire lives are the concrete expression of my prayer, my praise, my humility, and my charity.

I need priests who delicately and with intimate reverence occupy themselves with carving my divine image day after day on the countenances of those whom I have entrusted to them.

I need priests devoted above all to supernatural realities; through them I will animate all of human life.

I need priests who are spiritual professionals and not pretentious functionaries; who are kindly, patient, and above all have the spirit of serving and never confuse authority with authoritarianism.

In a word, I need priests who are deeply loving, who seek one thing and have one aim: that Love be more and more loved. (327)

October 31

Do you not know that in a few minutes I can cause you to gain hours in your work and souls in your activity? That is what is to be said to the world, especially to the world of priests, whose spiritual fruitfulness cannot be measured by their eagerness to produce but by the openness of their souls to the action of my Spirit. (328)

NOVEMBER

Do not try to complicate your spiritual life. Give your-self to me quite simply, just as you are. Be with me unclouded, unblurred, unshadowed. Then I can more easily grow within you and be received through you.
(149)

November 1*

Be sure that if I take up all the room I desire in the life, the heart, and the prayer of a priest, then he will have balance, development, and fullness of spiritual fatherhood.

How great and formidable is the soul of a priest! A priest is able to either perpetuate my presence and attract others to me or else, alas, to mislead and separate them from me, at times attracting them to himself. *(329–330)*

November 2

A priest without love is a body without a soul. More than anything, the priest should be given over to my Spirit, letting himself be guided by and acting through my Spirit.

Think of priests who fail in their ministry, many of whom have some excuse: lack of formation, of asceticism, of brotherly or fatherly support, or misuse of their capabilities. As a result they experience deception, discouragement, temptation, etc. . . . See me in each one. See me at times bruised and disfigured, but adore what there is of me in them and you will make my resurrection live again in everyone. *(331)*

---

*The thoughts for this month focus mainly on the priesthood. Many can be adapted to the situation of the person reading this book. They can also help us to pray for our priests. —Ed.

November 3

Only one group of priests truly sadden me: those whose work has made them become arrogant and hard. A thirst for power and a distorted sense of self have progressively emptied their souls of the deep love that should inspire all their attitudes and actions.

What bad things a hard priest can do! And what good things a kind priest can do! Make reparation for the former and support the latter. (332)

November 4

I forgive many things of a priest who is kind. I withdraw from a priest who has hardened himself. He has no room for me: I feel smothered in his soul.

Noises from within and without prevent many from hearing my voice and understanding the meaning of my appeals. That is why it is important to have in this overactive and frenzied world more islands of silence and calm where people can find me, converse with me, and give themselves freely to me. (333–334)

November 5

An environment of prayer is essential to make a country a Christian land, where what is best in men and women can develop. The teachers of prayer, above all, are the priests whose profound influence flows from their intimacy with me.

Offer me the sufferings of your brother priests often, sufferings of the mind, body, and heart. Unite them to what I suffered during my passion and on the cross. Pray that they draw out all their value of appeasement and coredemption in union with my suffering. *(335)*

November 6

Do not forget that redemption is first a work of love before it is a work of organization.

If only your brother priests were willing to believe that I love them—for without me they can do nothing—and that I need them to be among the people as much as my heart desires. *(337–338)*

November 7

I am in each of those consecrated women who have vowed their youth and their lives to the service of the mission of my Church.

I am there, the love of their hearts, the strength of their wills, and the light of their intellects. I am there, the life of their lives, the witness of their efforts and their sacrifices, working through them to reach souls. *(339)*

November 8

Offer me these living hosts [of consecrated souls] in whom I hide myself yet continue to labor, pray, and desire. Think of the thousands of women who have consecrated themselves to me. They have received the outstanding mission of continuing my Mother's action in the Church, to the extent they let themselves be permeated by me in contemplation.

What my Church currently lacks is not devotion or enterprising initiative, but the proper amount of genuine contemplative life. (*340*)

November 9

It is ideal for a consecrated soul to have a great deal of knowledge along with a great deal of love and humility. However, it is much more valuable to have a little less knowledge, with a great deal of love and humility, than a great deal of knowledge, with less love and humility. (*341*)

November 10

Ask me often to bring about in the world contemplative souls who, with a universal spirit, take over the role of prayer and expiation for many whose minds are closed to the appeals of my grace.

Recall that Teresa of Àvila contributed to the salvation of as many souls, as did Francis Xavier in his apostolic journeys, and Thérèse of Lisieux merited the title of Patroness of the Missions. (*342*)

November 11

Those who save the world are not agitators or theorists. The saviors of the world are those who, living intensely in my love, mysteriously radiate it on earth.

I am the High Priest. . . . When my divine Person became flesh in my Mother's womb, it took on human nature, and I consolidated in myself every spiritual need of humanity.

All men and women can and should be made part of this movement of sacralization, but the priest is the specialist, the professional, of the sacred. . . . If he works with a clear awareness of belonging to me, and if, at least as much as possible, he does everything for me and in union with me, then I am in him. I work with him to the glory of my Father in the service of his brothers and sisters. He becomes mine, my alter ego, and within him I myself draw people near him to my Father. (343)

November 12

Share my concern for my Church and especially for my priests. They are my "well-beloved," even those who, as a result of a storm, leave me for a while. I have great pity for them and for the souls entrusted to them. Yet, my mercy is inexhaustible if, through the prayers and sacrifices of their brothers and sisters, they come into my arms. They were marked in an extraordinary manner by their ordination, and even if they can no longer carry on a ministerial priesthood, their life, in union with my redemptive oblation, can be an offering of love that I will use. (344)

November 13

Take advantage of the time I leave you on this earth, the sole phase of your existence in which you can merit, to earnestly ask for more contemplative and mystical souls. They save the world and obtain for the Church the spiritual renewal it needs. *(345)*

November 14

Only those who find me in silent prayer, in humbly reading Holy Scripture, and in deep union can speak to me with competence. I am he who inspires their thoughts and speaks through their lips.

Priests and consecrated men and women must offer all the sufferings and all the agonies of humanity, in union with mine, for the life of the world. (346, 348)

November 15

If men and women only understood that I am the source of all virtues, of all holiness, of true happiness! Who better than my priests to reveal this to them, provided they accept being my close friends and live accordingly. This certainly requires some sacrifice, but it will soon be compensated for by fruitfulness and the serene joy that fills them. *(348)*

November 16

You must be willing to give me the time I ask of you. Has it ever been said that the faithful practice of devoting a single day exclusively to me has ever endangered one's ministry? *(349)*

November 17

It is no longer known how to perform penance, and that is why there are so few spiritual teachers and contemplative souls.

As much as I am against an overemphasis on suffering and the spirit of victimization, I also desire very much that there be no fear of the passing frustration brought about by a small sacrifice or a minor privation willed or accepted out of love. *(350–351)*

November 18

My word is ever true: "Unless you repent, you will all perish" (Lk 13:3). But if you are generous and attentive to my Spirit's suggestions, which will never harm your health or hinder the performance of your duties; if you are faithful and take part in the spiritualizing oblation that I will never cease offering in you, you will contribute to the cleansing of the sins of many. . . . You will obtain superabundant grace and . . . new types of saints will rise up, who will once more teach the secret of true joy to an astonished world. *(352)*

November 19

At Mass, through me and in my person, the priest changes the bread into my Body and the wine into my Blood.

In the confessional, he wipes away, by absolution, the faults of the repentant sinner through me, in my person.

The priest thinks, speaks, prays, is nourished, and expands through me, in my person. (353)

November 20

The priest no longer belongs to himself. He gave himself freely to me, body and soul, forever. That is why he would not know how to suddenly be as other men. He is in the world but is no longer of the world. By a special and unique title he belongs to me.

He must try to identify himself with me by communion of mind and heart, by sharing concerns and desires, by an ever-growing intimacy.

He must tend to express by his behavior something of my immense reverence for my Father and my inexhaustible generosity toward all people, no matter who they are.

He must ever renew the gift of his entire self to me, so that in him I might be fully what I desire to be. (354)

November 21

Many people let themselves become intoxicated by deceptive pleasure or seductive ideology. They become locked up in themselves and incapable of loyalty to me. I call them, but they do not hear. I try to draw them to me, but they have become impervious to my charms.

I urgently need consecrated persons. If they thought of gathering in themselves all the miseries of this mad world, if they thought of appealing to me for help in the name of all those whom the devil holds in chains, my grace would be able to overcome many obstacles more easily. (355)

November 22

Ask for more and more spiritual teachers, male and female. Such teachers made the restoration of the Church possible after the trials of the Reformation in the sixteenth century, and after the turmoil of the French Revolution. This, too, will bring about a new spring for the Christian community and will gradually prepare, despite all kinds of obstacles, an era of human brotherhood and progress toward unity.

This will not prevent men and women from living according to their era, from still being interested in the material problems of their times, but it will give them light and strength to influence contemporary public opinion and work out beneficial solutions. (357)

November 23

I invite everyone to come to me, but I desire to have certain men and women make my appeal heard. They must be drawn to me through the reflection of my face in the souls of my members, especially through consecrated men and women.

I want to reveal myself through their goodness, humility, kindness, receptivity, and the radiance of their joy. *(358)*

November 24

Words, of course, are necessary, along with useful structures, but what touches hearts is my presence, perceived and felt through one who belongs to me. A radiance emanates from me that is not deceptive.

More and more I expect this from you. As you are looking at me, contemplating me, my divine rays will penetrate and permeate you without your having to say a word. Yet when the occasion arises, your words will be charged with my light and become effective. *(359)*

November 25

My love for men and women is not returned. So often it is forgotten, ignored, rejected! Such blindness prevents minds from opening up to the light, and hearts from opening to my tenderness.

Fortunately, there are humble and generous souls of all ages in every country, every milieu of life. Their love makes reparation for a thousand blasphemies and a thousand rejections. *(360)*

November 26

The priest must be the first host of his priesthood. His offering must join mine for the benefit of the multitude. Whenever he fails to do this, a great loss occurs for many souls. Each time he does so patiently and lovingly, immediately a priceless growth of love for me occurs in this world. *(361)*

November 27

Trust in my power manifested in your weakness, which I turn into courage and generosity.

I love so much to see you spend an hour with me living in the Host. But do not ever come alone. Bring along all the souls I mysteriously link to yours and humbly make yourself a channel of my divine radiations.

Nothing is useless—not the least sacrifice, activity, or suffering—when lived in a state of self-offering.

Be more and more the host of your priesthood. A priesthood not in keeping with the oblation of the priest is a malformed priesthood. It is in danger of becoming barren and of obstructing my redemption. *(362)*

November 28

I will come to you "like a thief in the night" (1 Thes 5:2). I said this not to frighten you but out of love, that you may be always ready, and that you live each instant as you would wish to live the moment of your birth into eternal life.

If men and women looked at their lives more in death's rear-view mirror, they would see their lives' true meaning.

This is why death is not to be looked on in fear but with confidence, and why men and women must therefore recognize the full importance of the meritorious period of their life. (364)

November 29

Live on earth as if you had come from heaven. Be here below, the person who reenters from the beyond.

I let you still have a few more years on earth so you may lead a life filled with longing for heaven, a life in which the penetration of light from the Trinity is felt. (365–366)

November 30

Haven't I often given you testimonies of my solicitude? So then, what do you fear? I am always near you, even at the moment when everything seems to crumble, even—and especially—at the moment of death. Then you will see my arms embrace and clasp you to my heart. You will learn for what and whom your labors and sufferings have served. You will thank me for having guided you as I did, often preserving you from physical and moral dangers, leading you along unforeseen and at times disconcerting paths, while making your life a profound unity in the service of your brothers and sisters.

You will thank me, understanding how your God guided you and how he guides others. Your hymn of thanksgiving will unceasingly grow as you learn of the Lord's mercies toward you and toward the world. (367)

DECEMBER

I want your life to be a testimony of trust. I am the one who never deceives and who always gives more than he promises. (191)

December 1

Offer me the deceased that they may live from my life.

As if you had already arrived in heaven, pray, say hello, love, act, and enjoy yourself.

Think often about what our meeting in light will be. For that you were created, toiled, and suffered. A day will come when I will gather you in turn. Think about it often, and offer me in advance the hour of your death, uniting it to mine. (369–371)

December 2

Think often about what life after death will be like, the endless joy of a soul beaming with light and love, fully living the spirit of its whole being offered through me to the Father, and all the riches of divine youth received through me and coming from the Father.

Yes indeed, look on death with confidence and profit from your life's end by preparing for it with love.

Think of the death of your fellow humans, many thousands each day. How powerful for redemption this would be if it were offered to me! Do not forget: *oportet sacerdotem offerre* ("the priest must offer"). It is up to you to offer in the name of those who do not think of it. This is one of the most effective ways of making my sacrifice on Calvary worthwhile and of enriching your daily Mass. (372–373)

December 3

So many who do not suspect that I am going to call them tonight. . . .

Fall asleep in my arms at night. Thus you will die and arrive at paradise, at the great moment when we meet again.

Do everything keeping in mind the present moment. It will help you on many occasions to keep calm without impeding your enthusiasm. (374–376)

December 4

I consented to die out of love for you. You can give me no greater proof of love than to be willing to die in union with me.

[At the point of death] you will not be deceived. Overwhelmed by the majestic splendors you will find, you will have only one regret, that of not having loved enough.

Continue to unite your death to mine and offer it up to the Father through Mary's hands, under the influence of the Holy Spirit. (377–379)

December 5

In the name of your death united to mine, you can ask for immediate help to live the way of divine love better in the present moment. You can obtain everything in this way. So take advantage of it.

May your heart be increasingly open to my mercy. Humbly trust in my divine tenderness, which envelops you and imperceptibly makes your most ordinary activities fruitful, giving them a spiritual value that outlives them. *(379–380)*

December 6

What is the use of living, if not to love always more?

What is the use of dying, if not to eternally extend one's love and make oneself forever grow in it? *(381)*

December 7

My dear child, I gave you a presentiment of what the heavenly festival might be. What you dimly perceived it to be is nothing in comparison with the reality. You will see how I was and am a tender and loving God. You will understand why I have such great concern that men and women love one another, forgive one another, help one another. You will grasp the spiritualizing and purifying reason for patience and for undergoing suffering. *(382)*

December 8

[In heaven] your constant discovery of divine profundities will be an extraordinary and very exciting adventure. You will be imbued with my divinity, which will transfigure you and make you see all your brothers and sisters also transfigured in a mutual and exalted act of thanksgiving.

Believe me, the liturgical feasts on earth, which are celebrated for many reasons, are just the foretaste of the unending eternal festivals that keep souls simultaneously satisfied and constantly growing. *(382)*

December 9

Through my death I gave life to the world. Through the oblation of my death I can forever continue giving life to men and women. Yet I must have an abundance of deaths to overcome, without disregarding the free will, hesitation, and reticence of those who refuse to hear my call or who have heard it, but do not wish to let me enter into them. *(383)*

December 10

Heaven! I am heaven! According to the degree of your love, you will find infinite joy and will receive from the Father light and glory.

Then there will no longer be tears, suffering, ignorance, misunderstanding, jealousy, contempt, or meanness. There will be filial thanksgiving to the Holy Trinity and mutual acts of fraternal thanksgiving.

Of course, you will recall the lesser events of your earthly life, but you will see them in the synthesis of love through which they were transfigured and purified. *(384)*

December 11

How great and joyous will be your humility [in heaven]. It will make you as transparent as glass to all the reflections of divine mercy.

Yes, you will throb in unison with the beating of my heart and in harmony with the heartbeats of others, acknowledging the mutual benefits given to and received from benefactors. You will contemplate the small contributing role I will assign you for the happiness of all. *(384)*

December 12

Death does not take long for one who expires in an act of love and rejoins me in Light. Trust me. Just as I was there every moment of your life on earth, I will be there at the moment of your entrance into eternal life. My Mother too, who was so good to you, will be present—your sweet Mama. *(385)*

December 13

Think often of what you owe your friends in purgatory, who cannot by their own efforts raise themselves gradually up to the light. Do they not need one of their brothers and sisters on earth to merit what they would have obtained if before death they had made the choice of love that you make in their name? *(386)*

December 14

At the great moment of death, I promise the special grace of assistance to all who have lived for others before living for themselves. Doesn't love consist in this? Doesn't this living for others, expressed through small sacrifices, prepare one to die loving?

I know the hour of your death and how it will come about. But tell yourself again and again that I chose you, with all my love, to give your earthly life the maximum of spiritual fruitfulness. You will be glad to finally leave your body to enter into me. (387)

December 15

At the great moment of your final departure, even though you are unaware of it now, you will have all the grace you need with my presence. The measure of your love will cause you to fully cooperate with it.

You will die as you have lived. If you lived out of love, death will find you loving, and your last breath will be a breath of love. (388–389)

December 16

Having been your companion throughout your life, I am at the end of your road. Make always greater use of the time remaining to you before we meet again. At each hour, join me in prayer, share in my oblation, immerse yourself in my outpouring of love. Again and again seek my Spirit. Breathe him in and rejuvenate the beating of your heart. Does not my Spirit impart to you the love of your God? (390)

December 17

Let the thought of the heaven awaiting you fill you with joy amid suffering and make you hopeful amid the troubles of the present hour. Preach this hope to the discouraged.

Am I not with my Church until the consummation of the world? Instead of being discouraged, call on me: "Lord, save us! We are lost!" May faith increase in my presence and through my might. Then my tenderness and inexhaustible mercy will be made known. *(391)*

December 18

Your view of death must be a matter of faith. Our perception of heaven cannot respond directly to an experiential image, and that is why it is beyond every impression of the senses. This makes meritorious action possible during the earthly phase of your existence. What merit would you have if you knew everything now? Everything has its time. *(392)*

December 19

Your view of death must be a matter of trust. What you do not know by direct experience, you can know by relying on my word and trusting in me. I have never deceived you and am incapable of doing so. I am the Way, the Truth, and the Life. Everything I tell you of heaven will be even more beautiful than you can desire or conceive it to be. *(392)*

December 20

Your view of death must be a matter of love. Love alone enables you not to know but to have an idea of what I have reserved for you. This will be so much greater the more you have suffered and endured on earth. (392)

December 21

The light of glory is gorgeous. Participating in our Trinitarian joy is so blissful, it is above all else. The flame of love shines so brilliantly, you will be ignited by it in full communion with a universal and supreme love. If you had a true awareness of this, your life on earth would become impossible. . . . And how then could I have recourse to your free cooperation, meager though it may be, to work with me for the redemption and the progressive spiritualization of all humanity? (393)

December 22

If those about to die could only see the torrent of happiness that can engulf them from one moment to another, not only would they be unafraid, but how eagerly they would want to be with me.

These days you have thought a great deal about your life after death, and you have not neglected your earthly task on account of this. Do you not notice that thinking about the beyond gives life its true dimension in regard to eternity?

The same holds true for minor sufferings, deceptions, and annoyances—what are they in relation to eternity? In these present sorrows, minor and major, my universal work of redemption operates day after day, without your being aware of it. (394)

December 23

Live now by remembering and desiring your afterlife. It is the best benchmark of reality.

As you well know, death will be less a departure than an arrival, with more to be found than what was left behind. Death will be finding me in the light of my beauty, in the fire of my tenderness, and in the fervor of my gratitude. (395–396)

December 24

You will see me as I am and allow yourself to be fully absorbed in me, taking your place in the Trinitarian dwelling.

Then you will greet Our Lady, full of glory. You will see to what extent she is with the Lord and the Lord is with her.

You will express your boundless gratitude for her motherly treatment of you.

You will join your heavenly friends, from your guardian angel to all your earthly friends burning with love and illuminated by purest joy.

You will again find your sons and daughters according to the Spirit, and at the same time you will rejoice over what you owe to each one, from the least to the greatest members of my glorified Body. (396)

December 25

When the hour comes for us to meet again, you will understand how precious to my heart is the death of those who serve me and unite their death to mine.

It is the great means for reviving rebellious humanity and working for the spiritualization of the world. (397)

December 26

"If you abide in me and my words abide in, ask for whatever you wish, and it will be done for you" (Jn 15:7). Considering so many providential signs, don't you see how this is true?

I myself am in you: he who at times leads you counter to what appears to be normal and legitimate plans. The most complicated situations are solved at the right moment as if by magic.

Two conditions are required:
1. Dwell in me.
2. Listen to my words. (398–399)

December 27

You must think of me often, live more for me, be ever ready to serve me, gradually share everything with me, identify yourself more with me.

Furthermore, you must be aware of my real presence within you, a presence that speaks and at the same time is silent. You must listen to what I tell you without using words. *(400)*

December 28

I am the *Verbum silens* ("silent Word"), but I penetrate your mind with my ideas. If you are attentive, if you are recollected, my love will dispel the shadows in your thoughts and can then translate into words what I want to make known to you.

The intimacy you and I share is so strong that you can obtain everything for yourself from my might—for all those around you, for the Church, and for the world. This is how a contemplative person can make every activity fruitful, purified of all ambiguity, and profoundly fertile. *(400)*

December 29

May your life be permeated by true love, and may your death be preserved in love. This is the only thing that counts. For eternity, you will remain at the degree of love you will have attained. *(73)*

December 30

I love those long hours of sleeplessness during which you try to unite yourself to my prayer within you. Even if your ideas are confused, even if you find it difficult to find the words to express them, I read in your depths what you want to tell me, and in my own way, I speak silently to you.

At this moment, strive to be calm, to have understanding and kindness. May this be what is remembered about you.

You are at the hour in which the essential replaces what is urgent, and all the more so what is superfluous. Now what is essential is me and my freedom of action in the hearts of men and women.* *(175)*

December 31

"O Jesus, grant me to be in you and for you what you want me to be. Grant me to think in you and for you what you want me to think.

Grant me to say in you and for you what you want me to say.

Grant me to love in you and for you all those whom you give me to love.

Give me courage to suffer in you and for you with love what you want me to suffer.

Make me seek you always and everywhere in order that you may guide and purify me according to your divine will."† *(228)*

---

* Father Courtois wrote these lines two days before his death, which occurred during the hours of September 22–23, 1970. —*Ed.*

† Father Courtois turned to this prayer often in the final days of his life. He willingly shared it with others and recommended that they recite it each day. —*Ed.*

BOOKS & MEDIA

A mission of the Daughters of St. Paul

As apostles of Jesus Christ, evangelizing today's world:

We are CALLED to holiness
by God's living Word and Eucharist.

We COMMUNICATE the Gospel message
through our lives and through all
available forms of media.

We SERVE the Church
by responding to the hopes and needs
of all people with the Word of God,
in the spirit of St. Paul.

For more information visit our Web site:
www.pauline.org.

BOOKS & MEDIA

The Daughters of St. Paul operate book and media centers at the following addresses. Visit, call, or write the one nearest you today, or find us at www.paulinestore.org.

CALIFORNIA
3908 Sepulveda Blvd, Culver City, CA 90230   310-397-8676
3250 Middlefield Road, Menlo Park, CA 94025   650-369-4230

FLORIDA
145 S.W. 107th Avenue, Miami, FL 33174   305-559-6715

HAWAII
1143 Bishop Street, Honolulu, HI 96813   808-521-2731

ILLINOIS
172 North Michigan Avenue, Chicago, IL 60601   312-346-4228

LOUISIANA
4403 Veterans Memorial Blvd, Metairie, LA 70006   504-887-7631

MASSACHUSETTS
885 Providence Hwy, Dedham, MA 02026   781-326-5385

MISSOURI
9804 Watson Road, St. Louis, MO 63126   314-965-3512

NEW YORK
115 E. 29th Street, New York City, NY 10016   212-754-1110

SOUTH CAROLINA
243 King Street, Charleston, SC 29401   843-577-0175

TEXAS
No book center; for parish exhibits or outreach evangelization, contact:
210-569-0500, or SanAntonio@paulinemedia.com, or P.O. Box 761416,
San Antonio, TX 78245

VIRGINIA
1025 King Street, Alexandria, VA 22314   703-549-3806

CANADA
3022 Dufferin Street, Toronto, ON M6B 3T5   416-781-9131

¡También somos su fuente para libros,
videos y música en español!